PUBLISHED FOR THE MALONE SOCIETY BY
OXFORD UNIVERSITY PRESS

GREAT CLARENDON STREET, OXFORD OX2 6DP

Oxford   New York
Athens   Auckland   Bangkok   Bogota   Bombay   Buenos Aires
Calcutta   Cape Town   Dar es Salaam   Delhi   Florence   Hong Kong   Istanbul
Karachi   Kuala Lumpur   Madras   Madrid   Melbourne   Mexico City
Nairobi   Paris   Singapore   Taipei   Tokyo   Toronto   Warsaw
and associated companies in
Berlin   Ibadan

ISBN 0 19 729036 1

Printed by BAS Printers Limited, Over Wallop, Hampshire

THE TAMING
OF
A SHREW
1594

THE MALONE SOCIETY
REPRINTS, VOL. 160
1998

This edition of *The Taming of a Shrew* (1594) was prepared by Stephen Roy Miller and checked by R. V. Holdsworth and G. R. Proudfoot.

   The Society is grateful to the Huntington Library, California, for permission to reproduce its copy of the book (RB 69594).

March 1998   G. R. PROUDFOOT

INTRODUCTION

THE Stationers' Register for 2 May 1594 contains the following entry by the printer Peter Short:

Peter Shorte/ Entred vnto him for his copie vnder m^r warden Cawoodς hande/a booke intituled A plesant Conceyted historie called the Tayminge of a Shrowe . . . vj^{d1}

Three quarto editions of *The Taming of a Shrew* survive. This edition is a 1:1 photofacsimile based upon the unique copy of the 1594 printing now in the Huntington Library (RB 69594).[2] Short issued a page-by-page reprint in 1596 (Q2) with a virtually identical title-page, the imprint reading: 'Imprinred [*sic*] at London by P.S. and are to | be fold by Cuthbert Burbie, at his | fhop at the Royall Exchange. | 1596.' The Court book records a 'controu'sie' between Burby and Short in 1600 submitted to the settlement of two other printers on 7 September, but tells nothing of the cause or settlement.[3] Peter Short died in 1603. A Stationers' Register entry for 22 January 1607 records:

Mr Linge. Entred for his copies by direccõn of A Court, and wth consent of M^r. Burby vnder his handwrytinge These. iij copies. viž.
    Romeo & Iuliett.   Loues Labour Loste.   The taminge of A Shrewe   xviij^d R[4]

How the rights to *A Shrew*, first entered to Short, passed to Burby is not recorded. In 1607 Valentine Simmes published Q3 for Nicholas Ling. The device on the title-page is that of the publisher, Nicholas Ling, not that of the printer:

---

[1] W. W. Greg, *A Bibliography of English Printed Drama to the Restoration*, 4 vols. (Oxford, 1939–59), i. 10; there is a facsimile of this entry in S. Schoenbaum, *William Shakespeare: Records and Images* (London, 1981), p. 209 (item 103).

[2] Greg (item 120) provides printing details. The Malone Society wishes to thank the Huntington Library for permission to reproduce their copy from new photographs. *A Shrew* was not included in the volume of Huntington Shakespeare facsimiles edited by Michael J. B. Allen and Kenneth Muir, *Shakespeare's Plays in Quarto* (Berkeley, 1981).

[3] W. W. Greg and E. Boswell, eds., *Records of the Court of the Stationers' Company 1576 to 1602—from Register B* (London, 1930), 79.

[4] Greg, i. 22; Schoenbaum, 217 (item 126).

A | Pleaſaunt Conceited | Hiſtorie, called | *The Taming of a Shrew*. | As it hath beene ſundry times acted by the right | Honourable the Earle of *Pembrooke* | his Seruants. | [Device McKerrow no. 301] | Printed at London by *V.S.* for *Nicholas Ling*, | and are to be ſold at his ſhop in Saint | Dunſtons Church-yard in | Fleetſtreet. 1607.

Thereafter *A Shrew* appears once more in the Stationers' Register when rights are transferred from Nicholas Ling to 'John Smythick', now generally spelled 'Smethwick', on 19 November 1607 as number 9 in a list of 16 titles. John Smethwick's rights in *A Shrew* appear to have served the consortium printing the Shakespeare folio as authorization to publish Shakespeare's *The Taming of the Shrew*. Neither title was listed in the Stationers' Register entry for the First Folio made by Blount and Isaac Jaggard on 8 November 1623 which only sought to enter titles 'not formerly entred to other men' (Greg, i. 33). Smethwick's name appears in the colophon to the Folio, suggesting that his copyrights were available to the consortium, and when in 1631 he issued Q1 of *The Shrew* (printed by William Stansby) he adopted the Folio text instead of that of *A Shrew* which he had acquired in 1607. The 1631 title-page reads:

A WITTIE | AND PLEASANT | COMEDIE | Called | *The Taming of the Shrew*. | As it was acted by his Maieſties | *Seruants at the* Blacke Friers | and the Globe. | Written by Will. Shakeſpeare. | [Device McKerrow no. 376 (Smethwick's)] | *LONDON*, | Printed by *W.S.* for *Iohn Smethwicke*, and are to be | ſold at his Shop in Saint *Dunſtones* Church- | yard vnder the Diall. | 1631.

The most serious difficulty lying in the way of a printing analysis of Q1 *A Shrew* is the survival of only a single copy. This makes any search for broken or anomalous letters tentative since variations caused by the inking of a single run through the press cannot be refined by comparison and no press variants can be determined.[5] Close inspection has nevertheless provided a tentative history of the printing process.

Q1 of *A Shrew* is Peter Short's earliest extant play quarto. Short chose a large roman type, perhaps to disguise the shortness of the text or because he lacked another available fount. The lower case 'k' and 'w' often afford a weak impression. The text was set with an unjustified right margin, as if entirely in verse. Greg remarks: 'It is evident that a good deal of the text is really prose, while at the beginning of the conclusion even a direction [G2, lines

---

[5] This research was initially based upon photocopies provided by the Huntington Library which fortunately were clear. The evidence has been verified against Q1 independently by two Malone Society general editors, Richard Proudfoot and Roger Holdsworth.

1599–1602] has been printed as verse' (Greg, i. 203). This arrangement may reflect a decision to set the copy manuscript line for line, a procedure which would have allowed for greater accuracy in casting off copy for setting by formes. Evidence of a slavish following of copy lineation may be given by the shortness of some lines of the prose speech at 388–403 against the use of abbreviation to squeeze in the text of lines 395 and 397.

Little work on Peter Short as a printer has been published and virtually none on Short's printing of the two quartos of *A Shrew*. The Short editions of plays which have received most attention are his printing of the early version of Shakespeare's *King Henry VI, part 3*, entitled *The True Tragedy of Richard Duke of York*, in 1595 for Thomas Millington (in octavo format) and quires H through M of Shakespeare's *King Richard III* in 1597 for Andrew Wise: the first half was the work of Valentine Simmes. The next year, 1598, he appears to have printed for Andrew Wise two quarto editions of *King Henry IV, part 1*, though only one copy of quire C survives of the first (Q0).

Susan Zimmermann has published her findings on Peter Short's work, in 'The Use of Headlines: Peter Short's Shakespearian Quartos *1 Henry IV* and *Richard III*'.[6] Her references in this article to the printing of *A Shrew*, 1594, are limited to the claims that it was printed throughout with a single skeleton forme, a claim that is open to challenge.[7]

The quarto contains nine identifiable settings of the running title. The first three occur in gathering A, where two are used for the inner forme and all three for the outer. Four new running titles appear in both formes of sheet B and in the outer forme of sheet C, then vanish. An eighth setting joins the two from inner A in the inner forme of sheet C; the setting on C1^v of inner C is hard to identify but may be the setting used on A2^v. In any event, this running title is replaced by a ninth setting on D1^v and D2^v. The remaining three titles from inner C are used with this new running title for both formes of D through F and the final half sheet of G. It would appear that an initial intention to use two skeletons was abandoned after sheet C.

Identification of damaged letters is inherently difficult in view of reliance upon a single copy, but two distinctly damaged lower case roman letters, an 'n' and a 'y', appear to be used both in the outer forme of A (A2^v, 40 pla*y* and A3^r, 61 ho*n*our) and in the inner (A3^v, 115 M*y* and A4^r, 149 i*n*). No identifiable letters have been found in both formes of any other sheet.

[6] *The Library*, 6th series, 7 (1985), 218–55.
[7] A longer discussion of evidence for two compositors is given in Stephen Miller, *A Critical, Old-Spelling Edition of* The Taming of a Shrew, *1594* (Ph.D. thesis, Univ. of London, 1993), pp. 18–27.

As with the imposition, so with compositors, adequate evidence exists of a change of compositor at the beginning of quire D (or possibly around seven lines into D1^r, the first page of the inner forme of D, as discussed below, p. ix). It would appear that A2^r to the top of D1^r was set by one compositor and that a second, having taken over at D1^r, set the rest of the book. Evidence for two compositors consists of variations in spelling, typography of stage directions, punctuation, spacing of question marks, spacing of signatures and numbers and setting of speech prefixes as catchwords.

Some of the more obvious spelling variations are recorded in the following list:

form	A–C (1)	D–G (2)	form	A–C (1)	D–G (2)
Phy(i)lena	4	—	hir	25	6
Phy(i)lema	—	11	her	25	39
sirha	14	—	mistresse	10	1
sirra	—	16	mistris	—	15
sirray	—	2			
do	4	19	O	6	2
doo	28	13	Oh	3	8
here	9	32	son	1	21
heere	16	—	sonne	6	—
Saunder	5 [2]	—	souns	7	2
Saunders	[1]	—	sounes	—	10
Sander	2 [1]	5 [9]			
Sanders	—	[1]	Signior	2	—
[ ] = in stage directions			Signiour	2	—
			Senior	—	2
enough	3	1			
inough	—	5			

Quires A–C contain 723 lines (44.4% of the text), quires D–G, 904 lines (55.6% of the text and 181 more lines than A–C). Editors have found the variant spelling of the character name Phylena/Phylema significant and have generally preferred *Phylema* (Greek for *kiss*).

Variation between final '-l' and '-ll' spelling in the words *all, call, fall, pull, shall, tell, well*, and *will* shows stronger preference for the '-ll' form in D–G than in A–C.

> A–C (1)   D–G (2)

	A–C (1)	D–G (2)
-l	24	1
-ll	125	172

In total the first compositor used the final '-l' spelling in about one-fifth of the settings examined here. These are sometimes found in tight lines. Perhaps Compositor 1 was more willing to justify his lines by shortening '-ll' words than Compositor 2. Of the eight words ending in 'l' or 'll' just examined, the only use of a single '-l' after quire C is 'wel' at 725 on D1ʳ, a tight line. It may be worth mentioning that the spelling 'hir', preferred by Compositor 1, appears four times within the first seven lines of D1ʳ and only twice more in D–G. Both these observations might suggest that the stint of the first compositor continued for a few lines into D1ʳ. Against such speculation, however, are the occurrence in the first seven lines of D1ʳ of the spellings 'inough' (725) and 'sirra' (728) preferred by Compositor 2. The other evidence and logic suggest the beginning of quire D as the point of change. This mixture of spelling preferences in the first few lines of D1ʳ could result from the second compositor's brief, initial acceptance of copy spellings.

Stage directions in Q1 of *A Shrew* seem to observe a regular formula, being set in roman except for character names and Latin words—most often *'Exit/Exeunt'*—which are set in italic. Variations occur only in outer D (pages D1ʳ, D2ᵛ:D3ʳ, D4ᵛ). D1ʳ lacks stage directions; however a stage direction on D2ᵛ and the first two on D3ʳ are set entirely in italic. The remaining directions on D3ʳ are set in the standard formula found elsewhere in Q1. The use of initial italic *'S'* in the stage direction *'S*he beates him', (D4ᵛ:962) may be merely inadvertent. The stage directions in inner D follow the formula consistently, suggesting that it was set after outer D.

The three italic directions suggest that the second compositor began his stint setting stage directions in italic before conforming with the first compositor. Even then his conformity was not complete; a preference for setting stage directions in italic remains in respect of the conjunction 'and' between character names in stage directions, as these figures reveal:

> A–C (1)   D–G (2)

	A–C (1)	D–G (2)
roman 'and'	12	1
italic *'and'*	1	32

The sixteenth-century compositor was expected to punctuate the text he was setting. The distribution of semicolons and colons in Q1 of *A Shrew* suggests two hands:

A–C (1)   D–G (2)

	A–C (1)	D–G (2)
semicolons	4	2
colons	8	66

Because of type and inking difficulties some colons are difficult to determine securely, and the copy may have influenced the compositor's choice of punctuation to some extent, however increased use of colons beginning in D is clear.

The compositor of D–G seems to have been more liable than his colleague to end a speech with a comma or colon. In one two-page opening in outer F (F2^v:F3^r) three speeches end with commas (1363, 1376, 1421) and one with a colon (1395). Though this is untypical, other more scattered instances appear in the latter part of the quarto. The compositor of A–C ends only two speeches with commas—at 116 and 517.

Variation in the spacing of punctuation marks need not indicate a different compositor, but may do so if it is sufficiently systematic. Zimmermann attacks MacDonald P. Jackson for using as evidence the variation between spaced and unspaced ? in Short's quartos of Shakespeare's *Richard III* and *Henry IV, part 1*.[8] Similar variation is found in *A Shrew*. The figures, necessarily tentative as they are based on the evidence of a single copy, here suggest two compositors:

A–C (1)   D–G (2)

	A–C (1)	D–G (2)
spaced ?	44	8
unspaced?	13	54

Zimmermann is surely right to suggest that spacing evidence is not to be preferred to other evidence as to the division of compositorial stints—the amount of space between the end of a word and a question mark is sometimes difficult to determine exactly. In this instance, however, the evidence seems sufficient to corroborate the division of setting established on other grounds. The second compositor seems particularly reluctant to space before an italic question mark. There is only one clear example, at 769.

The signatures on A–C 2 and 3 use a space between letter and number.

[8] Zimmermann, 222; MacDonald P. Jackson, 'Two Shakespeare Quartos: *Richard III* (1597) and *I Henry IV* (1598)', *Studies in Bibliography*, 35 (1982), 173–90.

From D to E only signature 2 is signed. In F leaves 2 and 3 are both signed. In all these instances from D to F the space between letter and number is noticeably thinner than in A–C. The half sheet G is signed only on its first leaf.

Speech prefixes in Q1 *A Shrew* are notably regular. Prefixes which never vary in form are that for Ferando, which appears as '*Feran.*' 81 times, as well as '*San.*' (59 times), '*Aurel.*' (42), '*Lord*' (28), and '*Slie*' (26). Variation of some other speech prefixes, notably for Valeria: '*Val.*' (19), '*Vale.*' (4), '*Valer*' (1) seems not to relate to the pattern of composition.

The compositors do, however, differ when speech prefixes occur as catchwords. The first compositor always uses a full stop and abbreviates seven of nine speech prefixes used as catchwords. The second compositor uses the full form ten times, without punctuation in nine cases (the exception being '*Kate.*' on E4^r).

Speech prefixes are punctuated with a full stop in A–C whether or not they are abbreviated. The sole exception is '*Valer*' (468) which occurs on C1^r, where 2 of the 3 centered stage directions also lack final punctuation. In D–G eight unabbreviated forms are unpunctuated, a practice congruous with the setting of speech prefixes as catchwords by Compositor 2. (Speech prefixes without full stops after 468 are: *Kate*—773, 960, 974, 1075, 1532; *Slie*—1216, 1619; *Duke*—1401.)

These variations in spacing of punctuation, use of signatures, and setting of speech prefixes originated in Peter Short's printing house and were not influenced by copy. Such variations in Q1 *A Shrew* strengthen the evidence of spelling variation which suggests two compositors.

No author suggested for *A Shrew* has won general acceptance. Perhaps 'compiler' is a more apt term, as the text quotes and paraphrases more than one contemporary author. F. S. Boas collected references to Marlowe's work, particularly *Dr Faustus* and *Tamburlaine*.[9] Since the first known printed edition of *Dr Faustus* dates from 1604, the compiler must have had access to performances or manuscripts of the play.

Identified parallels listed below give through line numbers for *A Shrew*. Parallel texts referred to include the version of Shakespeare's *2 Henry 6* printed in 1594 as *The First Part of the Contention Betwixt the two Famous Houses of York and Lancaster* (*Cont.*), an English translation of lines by the French religious poet, Guillaume de Salluste Sieur Du Bartas, *La Création du Monde ou Première Sepmaine* (Du Bartas) and plays by Marlowe including

[9] *'The Taming of a Shrew' Being the Original of Shakespeare's 'Taming of the Shrew'* (London, 1908), pp. 91–8.

the A and B texts of *Doctor Faustus* (*Dr F*-A and -B), *Edward II* (*Ed 2*) and parts 1 and 2 of *Tamburlaine* (*1* and *2 Tam.*).[10]

9–10	*Cont.* 875–7
17–20	*Dr F*-B 227–31
125–7	*1 Tam.* 1.2.93–4
148–50	*2 Tam.* 1.2.9–11
185–7	*Ed 2*. 1.1.171–4
196–8	*1 Tam.* 3.3.117–20
237–9	*1 Tam.* 5.1.74–9
256–60	*2 Tam.* 2.4.83–9
[530, 537–8	*Dr F*-A 1233(?); 1243–4(?)]
593–5	*1 Tam.* 3.2.18–21
605–6	*Dr F*-B 169
661–2	*2 Tam.* 3.2.123–4 and *1 Tam.* 3.1.42–4
679–80	*1 Tam.* 1.2.87–9 and *2 Tam.* 1.1.111
687–90	*1 Tam.* 1.2.95–6 and 194–5
698–701	*Dr F*-A 361–3; -B 341–3
896–8	*2 Tam.* 4.3.12–16
1169–70	*Dr F*-B 597–9
1346–7	*Dr F*-B 1449–50
1548–57	Du Bartas, *Le Premier Jour* 19–26; 223–5

A Shrew is clearly related in some way to Shakespeare's *Taming of the Shrew* though scholars have disputed the manner for nearly three hundred years. Although *A Shrew* is only about sixty per cent the length of *The Shrew*, the plays share three plot strands: the taming of Kate plot, a subplot concerning the wooing of Kate's sister (or two sisters in *A Shrew*), and an induction introducing both plots as a play presented to the drunkard Sly by a lord. Structurally the two plays show numerous parallel features. Two key

[10] Reference for *Cont.* is to the Malone Society Reprint edited by William Montgomery, 1985; for Du Bartas *see* Urban Tigner Holmes, Jr., John Coriden Lyons, and Robert White Linker, eds., *The Works of Guillaume De Salluste Sieur Du Bartas: A Critical Edition with Introduction, Commentary, and Variants*, 3 vols. (Chapel Hill, North Carolina, 1935–40), ii. (1938), pp. 195, 202; parallels to works by Marlowe are quoted from Fredson Bowers, ed., *The Complete Works of Christopher Marlowe*, 2nd edn, 2 vols. (Cambridge, 1981) except for *Dr Faustus* A-text (1604) and B-text (1616) from W. W. Greg, *Marlowe's 'Dr Faustus' 1604–1616: Parallel Texts*, (Oxford, 1950).

characters, Kate and Sly, bear the same names in both plays. Verbally, however, the two plays are much less close than are other imperfectly parallel Shakespearian texts such as the early versions of *Hamlet*, *Merry Wives*, *Romeo*, *Henry V*, *2* and *3 Henry VI* (sometimes called 'bad' quartos) to fuller versions published later. *A Shrew* and *The Shrew* share parallel phrases, but rarely whole lines (the haberdasher/tailor scene contains some of the closest parallels: compare *A Shrew* 1063–1137 with Folio 2041–2179).

The Sly material forms a complete frame for *A Shrew*, rather than an induction only, with matter for Sly at both the beginning and end as well as interruptions during the whole course of the shrew play-within-a-play.[11] Of the three plot strands, the two taming plots are most clearly parallel. Also, intersections between the main plot and subplot are generally parallel. If the customary scene divisions of both versions are numbered sequentially, a comparative table reveals the structural parallels. The customary editorial act and scene numbering for *The Shrew* is given in parentheses.

Comparative analysis by scenes:

A Shrew	*The Shrew*
scene 1	scene 1 (Ind. 1)
scene 2	scene 2 (Ind. 2)
scene 3	scenes 3, 4, 5 (1.1, 1.2, 2.1)
scene 4	(parts of scenes 5,6), scene 7 beginning (2.1, 3.1, 3.2)
scene 5	scene 7 end (3.2) (otherwise no parallel)
scene 6	scene 8 (4.1)
scene 7	scene 9 (4.2)
scene 8	first part of scene 10 (4.3)
scene 9	scene 11 (4.4)
scene 10	second part of scene 10 (4.3)
scene 11	fragment of scene 9? (4.2) (otherwise no parallel)
scene 12	scene 12 (4.5)
scene 13	scene 13 (5.1)
scene 14	scene 14 (5.2)
scene 15	(no parallel scene)

Although the subplots of both plays are derived from Gascoigne's

---

[11] Possibly Shakespeare's *The Shrew* contained interruptions by Sly which were marked for deletion when act intervals were introduced into the text of *The Shrew* by the King's men sometime around 1609. *The Shrew* contains only one interruption by Sly, at a point where a missing division for Act two might be expected (F557–64). Gary Taylor and John Jowett discuss Folio act division in *Shakespeare Reshaped: 1606–1623* (Oxford, 1993), pp. 3–50.

Supposes, or possibly one or both versions of Ariosto's *I Suppositi,* of which Gascoigne's play is a translation, they differ radically from each other, and this fact lies at the heart of scholarly controversy over the relationship between the two versions.

On the evidence of his adoption of the play's epilogue into his edition of *The Shrew,* Alexander Pope apparently detected Shakespeare's hand in the additional Sly material of *A Shrew.* Editors followed suit until Malone, who maintained that *A Shrew* was Shakespeare's source. Peter Alexander challenged this theory in 1926, suggesting that *The Shrew* was the earlier text ('The Taming of a Shrew', *TLS* (16 Sept. 1926), 614).

Labelling *A Shrew* a 'bad quarto' of *The Shrew,* Alexander ascribed differences between the subplots to simplification by the compiler of *A Shrew,* who found himself incapable of reproducing Shakespeare's elaborate intrigue. In *The Shrew* the schemes to win Bianca include four competing wooers, one a 'pantalone' with no parallel in *A Shrew.* In *A Shrew* two men woo the shrew's two sisters without competition, although in both plays several points at which the two plots intersect, such as the visit of the tamer's friend to his house after the wedding, are parallel. Initially, several critics rejected Alexander's hypothesis. Duthie attempted to account for the divergent subplot of *A Shrew* by suggesting that it was a report of an early version which Shakespeare himself subsequently revised. Later twentieth-century critics have moved towards Alexander's view while accepting that no final critical agreement seems attainable.

Close examination of the subplot reveals an additional narrative element not found in *The Shrew,* which presents wooing couples of equal social rank. In *A Shrew* Aurelius, the wooer of one of the shrew's sisters, is a duke's son, higher in rank than Phylema, a fact which he conceals by disguising himself as a student. In a scene of wooing shared with Polidor and Emelia, the other sister, Aurelius administers a 'love test' to Phylema, asking whether she would not rather marry a duke's son than himself. He takes her refusal as his cue to marry her. Arriving unexpectedly, his father the duke protests at the indignity of his son marrying beneath himself, an issue which the arriving father, Vincentio, does not confront in *The Shrew* (5.1.122–4; TLN 2513–15). Such variations suggest less an incompetent compiler than someone engaged in deliberate revision or adaptation.

A clear instance of deliberate alteration between the subplots is found in the handling of one of the links between the intrigue subplot and the taming plot. Both versions provide the audience with a scene in which characters from the *Supposes* subplot comment that the tamer's home has become a 'taming school'.

Five lines in *A Shrew* (924–8) closely parallel *The Shrew* 4.2.51–4 (TLN 1903–7), the Folio scene in which Lucentio and Tranio inform Bianca that Hortensio has given up his suit for her—

The Shrew	*A Shrew*
	[*Aurel.*] . . .
Tra. I, and hee'l tame her.	And he meanes to tame his wife erelong.
Bianca. He sayes so *Tranio.*	*Vale.* He saies so.
Tra. Faith he is gone vnto the taming schoole.	*Aurel.* Faith he's gon vnto the taming schoole.
Bian. The taming schoole: what is there such a place?	*Val.* The taming schoole: why, is there such a place?
Tra. I mistris, and *Petruchio* is the master, (F1903–7; 4.2.51–4)	*Aurel.* I: and *Ferando* is the Maister of the schoole. (924–8)

In *The Shrew* the characters parallel to Aurelius and Valeria are Lucentio and Tranio, so some reassignment of speeches has taken place between versions to remove or add Bianca. The parallels are too extensive to be fortuituous and the reassignment of speeches can hardly be other than deliberate. This instance does not demonstrate which text has priority. It illustrates the impossibility of proving, exclusively on internal evidence, which text was written first.

Other verbal similarities close enough to serve as evidence for a connection between *A Shrew* and the Folio text may be found, for instance, at 8 (F4), 61 (F84), 116 (F153), 132 (F224), 326–7 (F446), 471–2 (F700–2), 656 (F1496), 864 (F1754), 890–2 (F1843), 946 (F2001), 974 (F2029), 979 (F2026), 988–9 (F2055–6), 1001 (F1956), 1075–7 (F2088–9), 1085 (F2114), 1087–90 (F2122–5), 1092–5 (F2117–20), 1097–8 (F2116), 1100–4 (F2108–12), 1110–17 (F2140–5), 1121–3 (F2152–4), 1136 (F2175–6), 1238 (F2323), 1319 (F2426–7), 1329 (F2473), 1468 (F2623), 1481 (F2630), 1482 (F2634), 1494–6 (F2644, 2646), 1502 (F2647–8), 1523–4 (F2658–9), 1543–5 (F2686–8), 1581 (F2669), 1585 (F2744). Indication of verbal parallels between the plays, using marginal references, was attempted in the Praetorius facsimile and in a parallel text edition edited by Albert R. Frey.[12] Given the brief, approximate and sometimes inconclusive nature of such verbal parallels, it has seemed better not to repeat their effort in this facsimile.

The profusion of borrowings from Marlowe and other texts found in *A Shrew* may be thought to provide the strongest circumstantial evidence that

[12] Charles Praetorius, ed., *The Taming of a Shrew, the First Quarto, 1594* (London, 1886); *The Taming of the Shrew: The Player's Text of 'The Taming of a Shrew' of 1594, with the Heminges and Condell Text of 1623*, Bankside Shakespeare 2 (New York, 1888).

the play's compiler might also have been a borrower from Shakespeare's *The Shrew*.

Henrietta C. Bartlett suggests the following provenance for the surviving copy of Q1: 'It has belonged successively to Malone, Inglis, Heber and the Duke of Devonshire. Hazlett [*sic*] says it probably belonged to A. Pope and was offered in Longman's Catalogue, 1817.'[13]

There are a few readings which may be unclear in the photofacsimile of Q1, but have been verified from direct, independent examination of the original by Richard Proudfoot and Roger Holdsworth:

91	*Boy*	927	ſchoole: (probably roman colon)
94	he	936	*Exennt* (First *n* is turned italic *u*)
137	*Sim.*	968	meate
289	faith	972	take
366	*Sannder* (first *n* is turned italic *u*)	972	ſhallbe
434	thee.	997	will
507	*Aureleus*	1019	liking
536	ſweet	1052	ſaies
591	loue: (probably roman colon)	1056	poſterities
657	were. (probably turned full stop)	1199	agree. (turned full stop)
731	Ile	1255	woman.
731	match. (probably full stop)	1323	knees,
773	pence (no punctuation)	1326	And
842	ſhrew	1356	me,
850	breeches	1485	Agreed:
905	ſportes	1490	maruell
907	*Cithereas*	1598	*Exit*
912	gaine	1622	had in

[13] *Mr. William Shakespeare: Original and Early Editions of his Quartos and Folio* (New Haven, 1922), p. 124.

TLN	Q1 reading	conjectural emendation
680	Apenis	Apenins[14]
690	forrowes	(*Q2–3* furrowes)[15]
985	vnto the thy	vnto thy
1028	in gots	(*Q2–3* ingots)
1095	Witha	With a[16]
1202	clad	(clads ?) *or is* And *an error for* To?
1252	*Cepherus*	*Cepheus*[17]
1347	hewd	hewe
1407	belong	(*Q2–3* be long)

[14] Presumably the compositor ignored a tilde over the 'i' (Richard Proudfoot). Marlowe's phrase 'snowy Appenines' (*2 Tam.* 1. 1. 111) may have influenced this line.

[15] The line imitates Marlowe: 'And Christian Merchants that with Russian stems | Plow up huge furrowes in the Caspian sea' (*1 Tam.* 1. 2. 194–5).

[16] Thomas Amyot, in the first reprint of Q1 (*The Old 'Taming of a Shrew' upon which Shakespeare Founded His Comedy*, 1844) records the 'a' as missing. Richard Proudfoot and Roger Holdsworth both testify to its authentic presence in Q1 now, as the facsimile shows, with no space separating it from 'With'. Proudfoot suggests: 'Amyot may have seen Q1 before restoration. The reading is "Witha" (unspaced). Recto of E2 has been patched, so that 2 letters on verso fall within the area of the patch, but they are *not* touched up in any way: [With(a b)ottome [the bowl only of the "b" is included in the area of the patch]]. The "a" could once have been on a torn or crushed flake of paper and thus invisible, but it's authentic.'

[17] In mythology *Cepheus* was father to Andromeda, mentioned in the following line. Both are constellations.

A
Pleaſant Conceited

Hiſtorie, called The taming
of a Shrew.

As it was ſundry times acted by the
Right honorable the Earle of
Pembrook his ſeruants,

Printed at London by Peter Short and
are to be ſold by Cutbert Burbie, at his
ſhop at the Royall Exchange.
1594.

A Pleasant conceited Historie, called
The Taming of a Shrew.

Enter a Tapster, beating out of his doores .
Slie Droonken.

Tapster.

YOu whorson droonken slaue, you had best be gone,
And empty your droonken panch some where else
For in this house thou shalt not rest to night.

          Exit Tapster.

Slie. Tilly vally, by crisee Tapster Ile sese you anon.
Fils the tother pot and alls paid for, looke you
I doo drinke it of mine owne Instegation,   *Omne bene*
Heere Ile lie a while, why Tapster I say,
Fils a fresh cushen heere.
Heigh ho, heers good warme lying.

       He fals asleepe.

Enter a Noble man and his men
from hunting.

Lord. Now that the gloomie shaddow of the night,
Longing to view Orions drisling lookes,
Leapes from th'antarticke World vnto the skie
And dims the Welkin with her pitchie breath,
And darkesome night oreshades the christall heauens,
Here breake we off our hunting for to night,

      A 2   Cuppel

Cupple vppe the hounds and let vs hie vs home,
And bid the huntſman ſee them meated well,
For they haue all deſeru'd it well to daie,
But ſoft, what ſleepie fellow is this lies heere?
Or is he dead, ſee one what he dooth lacke? (ſleepe,

Seruingman. My lord,tis nothing but a drunken
His head is too heauie for his bodie,
And he hath drunke ſo much that he can go no furder. 30

Lord. Fie, how the ſlauiſh villaine ſtinkes of drinke.
Ho, ſirha ariſe. What ſo ſound aſleepe?
Go take him vppe and beare him to my houſe,
And beare him eaſilie for feare he wake,
And in my faireſt chamber make a fire,
And ſet a ſumptuous banquet on the boord,
And put my richeſt garmentes on his backe,
Then ſet him at the *T*able in a chaire:
When that is doone againſt he ſhall awake,
Let heauenlie muſicke play about him ſtill, 40
Go two of you awaie and beare him hence,
And then Ile tell you what I haue deuiſde,
But ſee in any caſe you wake him not.

Exeunt two with *Slie*.

Now take my cloake and giue me one of yours,
Al fellowes now, and ſee you take me ſo,
For we will waite vpon this droonken man,
To ſee his countnance when he dooth awake
And finde himſelfe clothed in ſuch attire,
With heauenlie muſicke ſounding in his eares, 50
And ſuch a banquet ſet before his eies,
The fellow ſure will thinke he is in heauen,
But we will be about him when he wakes,
And ſee you call him Lord, at euerie word,
And offer thou him his horſe to ride abroad,

And

And thou his hawkes and houndes to hunt the deere,
And I will aske what sutes he meanes to weare,
And what so ere he saith, see you doo not laugh,
But still perswade him that he is a Lord.

Enter one.

Mef. And it please your honour your plaiers be com
And doo attend your honours pleasure here.

Lord. The fittest time they could haue chosen out,
Bid one or two of them come hither straight,
Now will I fit my selfe accordinglie,
For they shall play to him when he awakes.

Enter two of the players with packs at their
backs, and a boy.

Now firs, what store of plaies haue you?

San. Marrie my lord you maie haue a Tragicall
Or a comoditie, or what you will.

The other. A Comedie thou shouldst say, souns
thout shame vs all.

Lord. And whats the name of your Comedie?

San. Marrie my lord tis calde The taming of a shrew:
Tis a good lesson for vs my lord, for vs ȳ are maried men

Lord. The taming of a shrew, thats excellent sure,
Go see that you make you readie straight,
For you must play before a lord to night,
Say you are his men and I your fellow,
Hees something foolish, but what so ere he saies,
See that you be not dasht out of countenance.
And sirha go you make you ready straight,
And dresse your selfe like some louelie ladie,
And when I call see that you come to me,
For I will say to him thou art his wife,
Dallie with him and hug him in thine armes,
And if he desire to goe to bed with thee,

A 3

Then

Then faine some scuse and say thou wilt anon.
Be gone I say, and see thou doost it well.
. B. y. Feare not my Lord, Ile dandell him well enough
And make him thinke I loue him mightilie. *Ex. boy.*
   Lord. Now firs go you and make you ready to,
For you muft play afloone as he dooth wake.
   San. O braue, firha Tom, we muft play before
A foolifh Lord, come lets go make vs ready,
Go get a difhclout to make cleane your fhooes,
And Ile fpeake for the properties, My Lord, we muft
Haue a fhoulder of mutton for a propertie,
And a little vinegre to make our Diuell rore.
   Lord. Very well: firha fee that they want nothing.
                                        Exeunt omnes.

Enter two with a table and a banquet on it, and two
      other, with *Slie* afleepe in a chaire, richlie
      apparelled, & the mufick plaieng.
   One. So: firha now go call my Lord,
And tel him that all things is ready as he wild it.
   Another. Set thou fome wine vpon the boord
And then Ile go fetch my Lord prefentlie.   *Exit.*

Enter the Lord and his men.
   Lord. How now, what is all thinges readie?
   One. I my Lord.   (ftraight,
   Lord. Then found the mufick, and Ile wake him
And fee you doo as earft I gaue in charge.
My lord, My lord, he fleepes foundlie: My lord.
   Slie. Tapfter, gis a little fmall ale. Heigh ho,
   Lord. Heers wine my lord, the pureft of the grape.
   Slie. For which Lord?
   Lord. For your honour my Lord.
                                        Slie.

Slie. Who I, am I a Lord? Iesus what fine apparell
 haue *I* got.

Lord. More richer farre your honour hath to weare,
And if it pleafe you I will fetch them ftraight.

Wil. And if your honour pleafe to ride abroad,
Ile fetch you luftie fteedes more fwift of pace
Then winged *Pegafus* in all his pride,
That ran fo fwiftlie ouer the *Perfian* plaines.

Tom. And if your honour pleafe to hunt the deere,
Your hounds ftands readie cuppeld at the doore,
Who in running will oretake the Row,
And make the long breathde Tygre broken winded.

Slie. By the maffe I thinke I am a Lord indeed,
Whats thy name?

Lord. *Simon* and it pleafe your honour.

Slie. *Simon*, thats as much to fay *Si mi on* or *Simon*
Put foorth thy hand and fill the pot.
Giue me thy hand, *Sim.* am I a lord indeed?

Lord. I my gratious Lord, and your louelie ladie
Long time hath moorned for your abfence heere,
And now with ioy behold where fhe dooth come
To gratulate your honours fafe returne.

  Enter the boy in Womans attire.

Slie. *Sim.* Is this fhe?

Lord. I my Lord.

Slie. Maffe tis a prettie wench, whats her name?

Boy. Oh that my louelie Lord would once vouchfafe
To looke on me, and leaue thefe frantike fits,
Or were I now but halfe fo eloquent,
To paint in words what ile performe in deedes,
I know your honour then would pittie me.

Slie. Harke you miftreffe, wil you eat a peece of
 bread,

           Come

The taming of a Shrew.

Come sit downe on my knee, *Sim* drinke to hir *Sim*,
For she and I will go to bed anon.

Lord. May it please you, your honors plaiers be come
To offer your honour a plaie.

Slie. A plaie *Sim*, O braue, be they my plaiers?

Lord. I my Lord.

Slie. Is there not a foole in the plaie?

Lord. Yes my lord.

Slie. When wil they plaie *Sim?*

Lord. Euen when it please your honor, they be readie.

Boy. My lord Ile go bid them begin their plaie.

Slie. Doo, but looke that you come againe.

Boy. I warrant you my lord, I wil not leaue you thus.

Exit boy.

Slie. Come *Sim*, where be the plaiers? *Sim* stand by
Me and weele flout the plaiers out of their cotes.

Lord. Ile cal them my lord. Hoe where are you there?

Sound Trumpets.

Enter two yoong Gentlemen, and a man
and a boie.

Pol. Welcome to *Athens* my beloued friend,
To *Platoes* schooles and *Aristotles* walkes,
Welcome from *Cestus* famous for the loue
Of good *Leander* and his *Tragedie*,
For whom the *Helespont* weepes brinish teares,
The greatest griefe is I cannot as I would
Giue entertainment to my deerest friend.

Aurel. Thankes noble *Polidor* my second selfe,
The faithfull loue which I haue found in thee
Hath made me leaue my fathers princelie court,
The Duke of *Cestus* thrise renowmed seate,
To come to *Athens* thus to find thee out,

Which

160

170

180

8

Which fince I haue fo happilie attaind,
My fortune now I doo account as great
As earft did *Cæfar* when he conquered moft,
But tell me noble friend where fhal we lodge,
For I am vnacquainted in this place.

 Poli. My Lord if you vouchfafe of fchollers fare,
My houfe, my felfe, and all is yours to vfe,
You and your men fhall ftaie and lodge with me.

 Aurel. With all my hart, I will requite thy loue.

  Enter *Simon*, *Alphonfus*, and his
   three daughters.

But ftaie; what dames are thefe fo bright of hew
Whofe eies are brighter then the lampes of heauen,
Fairer then rocks of pearle and pretious ftone,
More louelie farre then is the morning funne,
When firft fhe opes hir orientall gates.

 Alfon. Daughters be gone, and hie you to y̆ church,
And I will hie me downe vnto the key,
To fee what Marchandife is come a fhore.

       Ex. Omnes.

 Pol. Why how now my Lord, what in a dumpe,
To fee thefe damfels paffe away fo foone?

 Aurel. Truft me my friend I muft confeffe to thee,
I tooke fo much delight in thefe faire dames,
As I doo wifh they had not gone fo foone,
But if thou canft, refolue me what they be,
And what old man it was that went with them,
For I doo long to fee them once againe.

 Pol. I cannot blame your honor good my lord,
For they are both louely, wife, faire and yong,
And one of them the yoongeft of the three
I long haue lou'd (fweet friend) and fhe lou'd me,
But neuer yet we could not find a meanes
How we might compaffe our defired ioyes.

    B   *Aurel.*

Aurel. Why, is not her father willing to the match? 220
Pol. Yes truſt me, but he hath ſolemnlie ſworne,
His eldeſt daughter firſt ſhall be eſpowſde,
Before he grauntes his yoongeſt leaue to loue,
And therefore he that meanes to get their loues,
Muſt firſt prouide for her if he will ſpeed,
And he that hath her ſhall be fettred ſo,
As good be wedded to the diuell himſelfe,
For ſuch a skould as ſhe did neuer liue,
And till that ſhe be ſped none elſe can ſpeed,
Which makes me thinke that all my labours loſt, 230
And whoſoere can get hir firme good will,
A large dowrie he ſhall be ſure to haue,
For her father is a man of mightie wealth,
And an ancient Cittizen of the towne,
And that was he that went along with them.

    Aurel. But he ſhall keepe hir ſtill by my aduiſe,
And yet I needs muſt loue his ſecond daughter
The image of honor and Nobilitie,
In whoſe ſweet perſon is compriſde the ſomme
Of natures skill and heauenlie maieſtie.

    Pol. I like your choiſe, and glad you choſe not mine, 240
Then if you like to follow on your loue,
We muſt deuiſe a meanes and find ſome one
That will attempt to wed this deuiliſh skould,
And I doo know the man. Come hither boy,
Go your waies ſirha to *Ferandoes* houſe,
Deſire him take the paines to come to me,
For I muſt ſpeake with him immediatlie.

    Boy. I will ſir, and fetch him preſentlie.

    Pol. A man I thinke will fit hir humor right,
As blunt in ſpeech as ſhe is ſharpe of toong, 250
And he *I* thinke will match hir euerie waie,
And yet he is a man of wealth ſufficient,

                           And

And for his person worth as good as she,
And if he compasse hir to be his wife,
Then may we freelie visite both our loues.

Aurel. O might I see the center of my soule
Whose sacred beautie hath inchanted me,
More faire then was the Grecian *Helena*
For whose sweet sake so many princes dide,
That came with thousand shippes to *Tenedos*,
But when we come vnto hir fathers house,
Tell him I am a Marchants sonne of *Cestus*,
That comes for traffike vnto *Athens* heere,
And heere sirha I will change with you for once.
And now be thou the Duke of *Cestus* sonne,
Reuell and spend as if thou wert my selfe,
For I will court my loue in this disguise.

Val. My lord, how if the Duke your father should
By some meanes come to *Athens* for to see
How you doo profit in these publike schooles,
And find me clothed thus in your attire,
How would he take it then thinke you my lord?

Aurel. Tush feare not *Valeria* let me alone,
But staie, heere comes some other companie.

Enter *Ferando* and his man *Saunders*
with a blew coat.
Pol. Here comes the man that *I* did tel you of.
Feran. Good morrow gentlemen to all at once.
How now *Polidor*, what man still in loue?
Euer wooing and canst thou neuer speed,
God send me better luck when I shall woo.
San. I warrant you maister and you take my councell.
Feran. Why sirha, are you so cunning?
San. Who I, twere better for you by fiue marke
And you could tel how to doo it as well as I.

B 2   *Pol.*

Pol. I would thy maister once were in the vaine,
To trie himselfe how he could woe a wench.

Feran. Faith I am euen now a going.

San. I faith sir, my maisters going to this geere now.

Pol. Whither in faith *Ferando*, tell me true.

Feran. To bonie *Kate*, the patientst wench aliue   290
The diuel himselfe dares scarce venter to woo her,
Signior *Alfonsos* eldest daughter,
And he hath promisde me six thousand crownes
If I can win her once to be my wife,
And she and I must woo with skoulding sure,
And *I* will hold hir toot till she be wearie,
Or else Ile make her yeeld to graunt me loue.

Pol. How like you this *Aurelius*, I thinke he knew
Our mindes before we sent to him,   300
But tell me, when doo you meane to speake with her?

Feran. Faith presentlie, doo you but stand aside,
And I will make her father bring hir hither,
And she, and I, and he, will talke alone.

Pol. With al our heartes, Come *Aurelius*
Let vs be gone and leaue him heere alone.   *Exit.*

Feran. Ho Signiour *Alfonso*, whose within there?

Alfon. Signiour *Ferando* your welcome hartilie,
You are a stranger sir vnto my house.
Harke you sir, looke what I did promise you   310
Ile performe, if you get my daughters loue.

Feran. Then when I haue talkt a word or two with hir,
Doo you step in and giue her hand to me,
And tell her when the marriage daie shal be,
For I doo know she would be married faine,
And when our nuptiall rites be once performde
Let me alone to tame hir well enough,
Now call her foorth that I may speake with hir.

Enter *Kate.*

Alfon.

12

Alfon. Ha *Kate*, Come hither wench & liſt to me,
Vſe this gentleman friendlie as thou canſt.

Feran. Twentie good morrowes to my louely *Kate*.

Kate. You ieſt I am ſure, is ſhe yours alreadie?

Feran. I tell thee *Kate* I know thou lou'ſt me well.

Kate. The deuill you doo, who told you ſo?

Feran. My mind ſweet *Kate* doth ſay I am the man,
Muſt wed, and bed, and marrie bonnie *Kate*.

Kate. Was euer ſeene ſo groſe an aſſe as this?

Feran. I, to ſtand ſo long and neuer get a kiſſe.

Kate. Hands off I ſay, and get you from this place;
Or I wil ſet my ten commandments in your face.

Feran. I prethe doo kate; they ſay thou art a ſhrew,
And I like thee the better for I would haue thee ſo.

Kate. Let go my hand, for feare it reach your eare.

Feran. No kate, this hand is mine and I thy loue.

Kate. In faith ſir no the woodcock wants his taile.

Feran. But yet his bil wil ſerue, if the other faile.

Alfon. How now *Ferando*, what ſaies my daughter?

Feran. Shees willing ſir and loues me as hir life.

Kate. Tis for your skin then, but not to be your wife.

Alfon. Come hither *Kate* and let me giue thy hand
To him that I haue choſen for thy loue,
And thou to morrow ſhalt be wed to him.

Kate. Why father, what do you meane to do with me,
To giue me thus vnto this brainſick man,
That in his mood cares not to murder me?

                She turnes aſide and ſpeakes.

But yet I will conſent and marrie him,
For I methinkes haue liude too long a maid,
And match him to, or elſe his manhoods good.

Alfon. Giue me thy hand *Ferando* loues thee wel,
And will with wealth and eaſe maintaine thy ſtate.
Here *Ferando* take her for thy wife,

                   B 3   And

And sunday next shall be your wedding day.

Feran. Why so, did I not tell thee I should be the man
Father, I leaue my louelie *Kate* with you,
Prouide your selues against our mariage daie,
For I must hie me to my countrie house
In hast, to see prouision may be made,
To entertaine my *Kate* when she dooth come.   360

Alfon. Doo so, come *Kate*, why doost thou looke
So sad, be merrie wench thy wedding daies at hand.
Sonne fare you well, and see you keepe your promise.

     Exit Alfonso and *Kate.*

Feran. So, all thus farre goes well. Ho *Saunder.*

    Enter *Saunder* laughing.

San. Sander, Ifaith your a beast, I crie God hartilie
Mercie, my harts readie to run out of my bellie with
Laughing, I stood behind the doore all this while,
And heard what you said to hir.   (wel to hir?   370

Feran. Why didst thou think that I did not speake
San. You spoke like an asse to her, Ile tel you what,
And I had been there to haue woode hir, and had this
Cloke on that you haue, chud haue had her before she
Had gone a foot furder, and you talke of Woodcocks
with her, and I cannot tell you what.   (for all this.

Feran. Wel sirha, & yet thou seest I haue got her
San. I marry twas more by hap then any good cunning
I hope sheele make you one of the head men of the
    parish shortly.   380

Feran. Wel sirha leaue your iesting and go to *Polidors*
The yong gentleman that was here with me, (house,
And tell him the circumstance of all thou knowst,
Tell him on sunday next we must be married,
And if he aske thee whither I am gone,
Tell him into the countrie to my house,
And vpon sundaie Ile be heere againe. *Ex. Ferando,*
              San.

San. I warrant you Maifter feare not me
For dooing of my bufineffe.
Now hang him that has not a liuerie cote
To flafh it out and fwafh it out amongft the proudeft
On them. Why looke you now Ile fcarce put vp
Plaine *Saunder* now at any of their handes, for and any
Bodie haue any thing to doo with my maifter, ftraight
They come crouching vpon me, I befeech you good M.
Saunder fpeake a good word for me, and then am I fo
Stout and takes it vpon me, & ftands vpon my pantofles
To them out of all crie, why I haue a life like a giant
Now, but that my maifter hath fuch a peftilent mind
To a woman now a late, and I haue a prettie wench
To my fifter, and I had thought to haue preferd my
Maifter to her, and that would haue beene a good
Deale in my waie but that hees fped alreadie.

Enter *Polidors* boie.

Boy. Friend, well met.
San. Souns, friend well met. I hold my life he fees
Not my maifters liuerie coat,
Plaine friend hop of my thum, kno you who we are.
Boy. Truft me fir it is the vfe where I was borne,
To falute men after this manner, yet notwithftanding
If you be angrie with me for calling of you friend,
I am the more forie for it, hoping the itile
Of a foole will make you amends for all.
San. The flaue is forie for his fault, now we cannot be
Angrie, wel whats the matter that you would do with vs.
Boy. Marry fir, I heare you pertain to fignior
    Ferando.
San. I and thou beeft not blind thou maift fee,
    Ecce fignum, heere.
Boy. Shall I intreat you to doo me a meffage to your
    Maifter?

                    San.

15

San. I, it may be,&you tel vs from whence you com.

Boy. Marrie sir I serue yong *Polidor* your maisters friend.

San. Do you serue him, and whats your name?

Boy. My name sirha, I tell thee sirha is cald Catapie.

San. Cake and pie,O my teeth waters to haue a peece of thee.

Boy. Why slaue wouldst thou eate me?

San. Eate thee, who would not eate Cake and pie?

Boy. Why villaine my name is Catapie,
But wilt thou tell me where thy maister is.

San. Nay thou must first tell me where thy maister is,
For I haue good newes for him, I can tell thee.

Boy. Why see where he comes.

Enter *Polidor*, *Aurelius* and *Valeria*.

Pol. Come sweet *Aurelius* my faithfull friend,
Now will we go to see those louelie dames
Richer in beawtie then the orient pearle,
Whiter then is the Alpine Christall mould,
And farre more louelie then the terean plant,
That blushing in the aire turnes to a stone.
What *Sander*, what newes with you?

San. Marry sir my maister sends you word
That you must come to his wedding to morrow.

Pol. What, shall he be married then?

San. Faith *I*, you thinke he standes as long about it as you doo.

Pol. Whither is thy maister gone now?

San. Marrie hees gone to our house in the Countrie,
To make all thinges in a readinesse against my new
Mistresse comes thither, but heele come againe to morrowe.

Pol. This is suddainlie dispatcht belike,
Well, sirha boy, take *Saunder* in with you

And

16

And haue him to the buttrie prefentlie.

    Boy. I will fir :come *Saunder.*

        Exit Saunder and the Boy.

    Aurel. Valeria as erfte we did deuife,

Take thou thy lute and go to *Alfonfos* houfe,

And fay that *Polidor* fent thee thither.

    Pol. I *Valeria* for he fpoke to me,

To helpe him to fome cunning Mufition,

To teach his eldeft daughter on the lute,

And thou I know will fit his turne fo well

As thou fhalt get great fauour at his handes,

Begon *Valeria* and fay I fent thee to him.

    Valer I will fir and ftay your comming at *Alfonfos*

      houfe.

        Exit Valeria

    Pol. Now fweete *Aurelius* by this deuife

Shall we haue leifure for to courte our loues,

For whilft that fhe is learning on the lute,

Hir fifters may take time to fteele abrode,

For otherwife fhele keep them both within,

And make them worke whilft fhe hir felfe doth play,

But come lets go vnto *Alfonfos* houfe,

And fee how *Valeria* and *Kate* agreefe,

I doute his Mufick skarfe will pleafe his skoller,

But ftay here comes *Alfonfo.*

        Enter *Alfonfo*

    Alfonfo. What M. *Polidor* you are well mett,

I thanke you for the man you fent to me,

A good Mufition I thinke he is,

I haue fet my daughter and him togither,

But is this gentellman a frend of youres?

    Pol. He is, I praie you fir bid him welcome,

He's a wealthie Marchants fonne of *Ceftus.*

    Alfonfo. Your welcom fir and if my houfe aforde

              C   You

You any thing that may content your mind,   490
I pray you fir make bold with me.

 Aurel. I thanke you fir, and if what I haue got,
By marchandife or trauell on the feas,
Sattins or lawnes or azure colloured filke,
Or pretious firie pointed ftones of Indie,
You fhall command both them my felfe and all.

 Alfon. Thanks gentle fir, *Polidor* take him in,
And bid him welcome to vnto my houfe,
For thou I thinke muft be my fecond fonne,   500
Ferando, Polidor dooft thou not know
Muft marry *Kate*, and to morrow is the day.

 Pol. Such newes I heard, and *I* came now to know.

 Alfon. *Polidor* tis true, goe let me alone,
For I muft fee againft the bridegroome come,
That all thinges be according to his mind,
And fo Ile leaue you for an houre or two. *Exit.*

 Pol. Come then *Aurelus* come in with me,
And weele go fit a while and chat with them,
And after bring them foorth to take the aire. *Exit.*   510
   Then *Slie* fpeakes.

 Slie. *Sim*, when will the foole come againe?

 Lord. Heele come againe my Lord anon.

 Slie. Gis fome more drinke here, founs wheres
The Tapfter, here *Sim* eate fome of thefe things.

 Lord. So I doo my Lord.

 Slie. Here *Sim*, I drinke to thee.

 Lord. My Lord heere comes the plaiers againe,

 Slie. O braue, heers two fine gentlewomen.

  Enter *Valeria* with a Lute and *Kate*
    with him.   520

 Vale. The fencelefse trees by mufick haue bin moou'd
And at the found of pleafant tuned ftrings,

       Haue

Haue ſauage beaſtes hung downe their liſtning heads,
As though they had beene caſt into a trance.
Then it may be that ſhe whom nought can pleaſe,
With muſickes ſound in time may be ſurpriſde,
Come louely miſtreſſe will you take your lute,
And play the leſſon that I taught you laſt?

   Kate. It is no matter whether I doo or no,
For truſt me I take no great delight in it.

   Vale. I would ſweet miſtreſſe that it laie in me,
To helpe you to that thing thats your delight.

   Kate. In you with a peſtlence, are you ſo kind?
Then make a night cap of your fiddles caſe,
To warme your head, and hide your filthie face.

   Val. If that ſweet miſtreſſe were your harts content,
You ſhould command a greater thing then that,
Although it were ten times to my diſgrace.

   Kate. Your ſo kind twere pittie you ſhould be
      hang'd,
And yet methinkes the foole dooth looke aſquint.

   Val. Why miſtreſſe doo you mocke me ?

   Kate. No, but I meane to moue thee.

   Val. Well, will you plaie a little ?

   Kate. I, giue me the Lute.
           She plaies.

   Val. That ſtop was falſe, play it againe.

   Kate. Then mend it thou, thou filthy aſſe.

   Val. What, doo you bid me kiſſe your arſe ?

   Kate. How now iack ſauſe, your a iollie mate,
Your beſt be ſtill leaſt I croſſe your pate,
And make your muſicke flie about your eares,
Ile make it and your fooliſh coxcombe meet.
      She offers to ſtrike him with the lute.

   Val. Hold miſtreſſe, ſouns wil you breake my lute ?

   Kate. I on thy head, and if thou ſpeake to me,

             C 2   There

There take it vp and fiddle ſomewhere elſe,
She throwes it downe.
And ſee you come no more into this place,
Leaſt that I clap your fiddle on your face.   *Ex. Kate.*   560

  Val. Souns, teach hir to play vpon the lute?
The deuill ſhal teach her firſt, I am glad ſhees gone,
For I was neare ſo fraid in all my life,
But that my lute ſhould flie about mine eares,
My maiſter ſhall teach her his ſelfe for me,
For Ile keepe me far enough without hir reach,
For he and *Polydor* ſent me before
To be with her and teach her on the lute,
Whilſt they did court the other gentlewomen,
And heere methinkes they come togither.   570

Enter *Aurelius, Polidor, Emelia,*
and *Philena.*

  Pol. How now *Valeria,* whears your miſtreſſe?
  Val. At the vengeance I thinke and no where elſe.
  Aurel. Why *Valeria,* will ſhe not learne apace?
  Val. Yes berlady ſhe has learnt too much already,
And that I had felt had I not ſpoke hir faire,
But ſhe ſhall neare be learnt for me againe.
  Aurel. Well *Valeria* go to my chamber,
And beare him companie that came to daie   580
From *Ceſtus,* where our aged father dwels.   *Ex. Valeria.*
  Pol. Come faire *Emelia* my louelie loue,
Brighter then the burniſht paſſace of the ſunne,
The eie-ſight of the glorious firmament,
In whoſe bright lookes ſparkles the radiant fire,
Wilie *Prometheus* ſlilie ſtole from *Ioue,*
Infuſing breath, life, motion, ſoule,
To euerie obiect ſtriken by thine eies.
Oh faire *Emelia* I pine for thee,
And either muſt enioy thy loue, or die.   590

Emelia.

Eme. Fie man, I know you will not die for loue,
Ah *Polidor* thou needft not to complaine,
Eternall heauen fooner be diffolude,
And all that pearfeth Phebus filuer eie,
Before fuch hap befall to *Polidor*.

Pol. Thanks faire *Emelia* for thefe fweet words,
But what faith *Phylena* to hir friend?

Phyle. Why I am buying marchandife of him.

Aurel. Miftreffe you fhall not need to buie of me,
For when I croft the bubling Canibey,
And failde along the Criftall Helifpont,
I filde my cofers of the wealthie mines,
Where I did caufe Millions of labouring Moores
To vndermine the cauernes of the earth,
To feeke for ftrange and new found pretious ftones,
And diue into the fea to gather pearle,
As faire as *Iuno* offered *Priams* fonne,
And you fhall take your liberall choice of all.

Phyle. I thanke you fir and would *Phylena* might
In any curtefie requite you fo,
As fhe with willing hart could well beftow.

Enter *Alfonso*.

Alfon. How now daughters, is *Ferando* come?

Eme. Not yet father, I wonder he ftaies fo long.

Alfon. And wheres your fifter that fhe is not heere?

Phyle. She is making of hir readie father
To goe to church and if that he were come.

Pol. I warrant you heele not be long awaie.

Alfon. Go daughters get you in, and bid your
Sifter prouide her felfe againft that we doo come,
And fee you goe to church along with vs.

Exit Philena and *Emelia*.

I maruell that *Ferando* comes not away.

C 3   Pol.

Pol. His Tailor it may be hath bin too flacke,
In his apparrell which he meanes to weare,
For no queftion but fome fantafticke futes
He is determined to weare to day,
And richly powdered with pretious ftones,
Spotted with liquid gold, thick fet with pearle,
And fuch he meanes fhall be his wedding futes.

Alfon. I carde not I what coft he did beftow,
In gold or filke, fo he himfelfe were heere,
For I had rather lofe a thoufand crownes,
Then that he fhould deceiue vs heere to daie,
But foft I thinke I fee him come.

Enter *Ferando* bafelie attired, and a
red cap on his head.

Feran. Godmorow father, *Polidor* well met,
You wonder I know that I haue ftaid fo long.

Alfon. I marrie fon, we were almoft perfwaded,
That we fhould fcarfe haue had our bridegroome heere,
But fay, why art thou thus bafely attired?

Feran. Thus richlie father you fhould haue faid,
For when my wife and I am married once,
Shees fuch a fhrew, if we fhould once fal out,
Sheele pul my coftlie futes ouer mine eares,
And therefore am I thus attired awhile,
For manie thinges I tell you's in my head,
And none muft know thereof but *Kate* and *I*,
For we fhall liue like lammes and Lions fure,
Nor lammes to Lions neuer was fo tame,
If once they lie within the Lions pawes
As *Kate* to me if we were married once,
And therefore come let vs to church prefently.

Pol. Fie *Ferando* not thus atired for fhame,
Come to my Chamber and there fute thy felfe,

Of

630

640

650

Of twentie sutes that I did neuer were·

   Feran. Tush *Polidor* I haue as many sutes
Fantasticke made to fit my humor so
As any in Athens and as richlie wrought
As was the Massie Robe that late adornd,
The stately legate of the Persian King,
And this from them haue I made choise to weare.

   Alfon. I prethie *Ferando* let me intreat
Before thou goste vnto the church with vs,
To put some other sute vpon thy backe.

   Feran. Not for the world if I might gaine it so,
And therefore take me thus or not at all,

               Enter *Kate.*

But soft se where my *Kate* doth come,
I must salute hir: how fares my louely *Kate?*
What art thou readie? shall we go to church.?

   Kate. Not I with one so mad, so basely tirde,
To marrie such a filthie slauish groome,
That as it seemes sometimes is from his wits,
Or else he would not thus haue come to vs.

   Feran. Tush *Kate* these words addes greater loue in me
And makes me thinke thee fairrer then before,
Sweete *Kate* the louelier then Dianas purple robe,
Whiter then are the snowie Apenis,
Or icie haire that groes on Boreas chin.
Father I sweare by Ibis golden beake,
More faire and Radiente is my bonie *Kate*,
Then siluer Zanthus when he doth imbrace,
The ruddie Simies at Idas feete,
And care not thou swete *Kate* how I be clad,
Thou shalt haue garments wrought of Median silke,
Enchast with pretious Iewells fecht from far,
By Italian Marchants that with Russian stemes,
Plous vp huge sorrowes in the *Terren Maine*,

                        And

And better farre my louely *Kate* shall weare,
Then come sweet loue and let vs to the church,
For this I sweare shall be my wedding suite.

        Exeunt omnes.

Alfon. Come gentlemen go along with vs,
For thus doo what we can he will be wed. *Exit.*

    Enter *Polidors* boy and *Sander.*
 Boy. Come hither sirha boy.
 San. Boy; oh disgrace to my person, souns boy
Of your face, you haue many boies with such
Pickadeuantes I am sure, souns would you
Not haue a bloudie nose for this?
 Boy. Come, come, I did but iest, where is that
Same peece of pie that I gaue thee to keepe.
 San. The pie? I you haue more minde of your bellie
Then to go see what your maister dooes.
 Boy. Tush tis no matter man I prethe giue it me,
I am verie hungry I promise thee.
 San. Why you may take it and the deuill burst
You with it, one cannot saue a bit after supper,
But you are alwaies readie to munch it vp.
 Boy. Why come man, we shall haue good cheere
Anon at the bridehouse, for your maisters gone to
Church to be married alreadie, and thears
Such cheere as passeth.
 San. O braue, I would I had eate no meat this weeke,
For I haue neuer a corner left in my bellie
To put a venson pastie in, I thinke I shall burst my selfe
With eating, for Ile so cram me downe the tarts
And the marchpaines, out of all crie.
 Boy. I, but how wilt thou doo now thy maisters
Matried, thy mistresse is such a deuill, as sheele make
Thee forget thy eating quickly, sheele beat thee so.

           San.

700

710

720

San. Let my maister alone with hir for that, for
Heele make hir tame wel inough ere longe I warent thee
For he's such a churle waxen now of late that and he be
Neuer so little angry he thums me out of all crie,
But in my minde sirra the yongest is a verie
Prettie wench, and if I thought thy maister would
Not haue hir I de haue a flinge at hir
My selfe, I'e see soone whether twill be a match.
Or no: and it will not Ile set the matter
Hard for my selfe I warrant thee.

    Boy. Sounes you slaue will you be a Riuall with
My maister in his loue, speake but such
Another worde and Ile cut off one of thy legges.

    San. Oh, cruell iudgement, nay then sirra,
My tongue shall talke no more to you, marry my
Timber shall tell the trustie message of his maister,
Euen on the very forehead on thee, thou abusious
Villaine, therefore prepare thy selfe.

    Boy. Come hither thou Imperfecksious slaue in
Regard of thy beggery, holde thee theres
Two shillings for thee? to pay for the
Healing of thy left legge which I meane
Furiously to inuade or to maime at the least.

    San. O supernodicall foule? well Ile take your
two shillinges but Ile barre striking at legges.

    Boy. Not I, for Ile strike any where.

    San. Here here take your two shillings again
Ile see thee hangd ere Ile fight with thee,
I gat a broken shin the other day,
Tis not, whole yet and therefore Ile not fight
Come come why should we fall out?

    Boy. Well sirray your faire words hath something
Alaied my Coller: I am content for this once
To put it vp and be frends with thee,

D

But

But soft see where they come all from church,
Belike they be Married allredy.

Enter *Ferando and Kate and Alfonso and Polidor*
and Emelia and Aurelius and Philema.   760

Feran. Father farwell, my *Kate* and I must home,
Sirra go make ready my horse presentlie.

Alfon. Your horse! what son I hope you doo but iest,
I am sure you will not go so suddainly.

Kate. Let him go or tarry I am resolu'de to stay,
And not to trauell on my wedding day.

Feran. Tut *Kate* I tell thee we must needes go home,
Villaine hast thou saddled my horse?

San. Which horse, your curtall?   770

Feran. Sounes you slaue stand you prating here?
Saddell the bay gelding for your Mistris.

Kate Not for me: for Ile not go.   (pence

San. The ostler will not let me haue him, you owe ten
For his meate, and *6* pence for stuffing my mistris saddle.

Feran. Here villaine go pay him straight.

San. Shall I giue them another pecke of lauender.

Feran. Out slaue and bring them presently to the dore

Alfon. Why son I hope at least youle dine with vs.

San. I pray you maister lets stay till dinner be don.

Feran. Sounes villaine art thou here yet? *Ex. Sander.* 780
Come *Kate* our dinner is prouided at home.

Kate. But not for me, for here I meane to dine.
Ile haue my will in this as well as you,
Though you in madding mood would leaue your frends
Despite of you Ile tarry with them still.

Feran. I *Kate* so thou shalt but at some other time,
When as thy sisters here shall be espousd,
Then thou and I will keepe our wedding day,
In better sort then now we can prouide,   790

For

26

For here *I* promiſe thee before them all,
We will ere long returne to them againe,
Come *Kate* ſtand not on termes we will awaie,
This is my day, to morrow thou ſhalt rule,
And I will doo what euer thou commandes.
Gentlemen farwell, wele take our leues,
It will be late before that we come home.

    Exit Ferando and Kate.

 Pol. Farwell *Ferando* ſince you will be gone.
 Alfon. So mad a cupple did I neuer ſee.
 Emel. They're euen as well macht as I would wiſh.
 Phile. And yet I hardly thinke that he can tame her.
For when he has don ſhe will do what ſhe liſt.
 Aurel. Her manhood then is good I do beleeue.
 Pol. Aurelius or elſe I miſſe my marke,
Her toung will walke if ſhe doth hold her handes,
I am in dout ere halfe a month be paſt
Hele curſe the prieſt that married him ſo ſoone,
And yet it may be ſhe will be reclaimde,
For ſhe is verie patient grone of late.
 Alfon. God hold it that it may continue ſtill,
I would be loth that they ſhould diſagree,
But he I hope will holde her in a while.
 Pol. Within this two daies I will ride to him,
And ſee how louingly they do agree.
 Alfon. Now *Aurelius* what ſay you to this,
What haue you ſent to *Ceſtus* as you ſaid,
To certifie your father of your loue,
For I would gladlie he would like of it,
And if he be the man you tell to me,
I geſſe he is a Marchant of great wealth.
And I haue ſeene him oft at *Athens* here,
And for his ſake aſſure thee thou art welcome.
 Pol. And ſo to me whileſt *Polidor* doth liue.

   D 2   *Aurelius*

Aurel. I find it so right worthie gentlemen,
And of what worth your frendship I esteme,
I leue censure of your seuerall thoughts,
But for requitall of your fauours past,
Rests yet behind, which when occasion serues
I vow shalbe remembred to the full,
And for my fathers comming to this place,
I do expect within this weeke at most.

   Alfon. Inough *Aurelieus?* but we forget
Our Marriage dinner now the bride is gon,
Come let vs se what there they left behind.   *Exit Omnes*

     Enter Sanders with two or three
        seruing men

  San. Come sirs prouide all thinges as fast as you can,
For my Masters hard at hand and my new Mistris
And all, and he sent me before to see all thinges redy.

  Tom. Welcome home *Sander* sirra how lookes our
New Mistris they say she's a plagie shrew.

  San. I and that thou shalt find I can tell thee and thou
Dost not please her well, why my Maister
Has such a doo with hir as it passeth and he's euen
like a madman.

  Will. Why *Sander* what dos he say.

  San. Why Ile tell you what: when they should
Go to church to be maried he puts on an olde
Ierkin and a paire of canuas breeches downe to the
Small of his legge and a red cap on his head and he
Lookes as thou wilt burst thy selfe with laffing
When thou seest him: he's ene as good as a
Foole for me: and then when they should go to dinner
He made me Saddle the horse and away he came.
And nere tarried for dinner and therefore you had best
Get supper reddy against they come, for

                    They

830

840

850

They be hard at hand *I* am sure by this time.

    Tom. Sounes see where they be all redy.

          Enter Ferando and Kate.

    Feran. Now welcome *Kate*: wher᷉es these villains

Here, what? not supper yet vppon the borde:

Nor table spred nor nothing don at all,

Wheres that villaine that I sent before.

    San. Now, *adsum*, sir.

    Feran. Come hether you villaine Ile cut your nose,

You Rogue: helpe me of with my bootes: wilt please

You to lay the cloth? sounes the villaine

Hurts my foote? pull easely I say; yet againe.

          He beates them all.

      They couer the bord and fetch in the meate.

Sounes? burnt and skorcht who drest this meate?

    Will. Forsouth Iohn cooke.

          He throwes downe the table and meate

            and all, and beates them.

    Feran. Go you villaines bringe you me such meate,

Out of my sight I say and beare it hence,

Come *Kate* wele haue other meate prouided,

Is there a fire in my chamber sir?

    San. I forsooth.   *Exit Ferando and Kate.*

    Manent seruingmen and eate vp all the meate.

    Tom. Sounes? I thinke of my conscience my Masters

Mad since he was maried.

    Will. I last what a boxe he gaue *Sander*

For pulling of his bootes.

          Enter *Ferando* againe.

    San. I hurt his foote for the nonce man.

    Feran. Did you so you damned villaine.

          He beates them all out againe.

This humor must I holde me to a while,

                        To

To bridle and hold backe my headstrong wife,
With curbes of hunger: ease: and want of sleepe,
Nor sleepe nor meate shall she inioie to night,
Ile mew her vp as men do mew their hawkes,
And make her gentlie come vnto the lure,
Were she as stuborne or as full of strength
As were the *Thracian* horse *Alcides* tamde,
That King *Egeus* fed with flesh of men,
Yet would I pull her downe and make her come
As hungry hawkes do flie vnto there lure.   **Exit.**   900

   Enter *Aurelius and Valeria.*
  Aurel. Valeria attend: I haue a louely loue,
As bright as is the heauen cristalline,
As faire as is the milke white way of Ioue,
As chast as *Phœbe* in her sommer sportes,
As softe and tender as the asure downe,
That circles *Cithereas* siluer doues.
Her do *I* meane to make my louely bride,
And in her bed to breath the sweete content,
That *I* thou knowst long time haue aimed at.   910
Now *Valeria* it rests in thee to helpe
To compasse this, that *I* might gaine my loue,
Which easilie thou maist performe at will,
If that the marchant which thou toldst me of,
Will as he sayd go to *Alfonsos* house,
And say he is my father, and there with all
Pas ouer certaine deedes of land to me,
That I thereby may gaine my hearts desire,
And he is promised reward of me.
  Val. Feare not my Lord Ile fetch him straight to you,   920
For hele do any thing that you command,
But tell me my Lord, is *Ferando* married then?
  Aurel. He is: and *Polidor* shortly shall be wed,
And he meanes to tame his wife erelong.

           Valeria

The taming of a Shrew.

Vale. He saies so.

Aurel. Faith he's gon vnto the taming schoole.

Val. The taming schoole: why is there such a place?

Aurel. I: and *Ferando* is the Maister of the schoole.

Val. Thats rare: but what *decorum* dos he vse?

Aurel. Faith I know not: but by som odde deuise
Or other, but come *Valeria* I long to see the man,
By whome we must comprise our plotted drift,
That I may tell him what we haue to doo.

   Val. Then come my Lord and I will bring you to him
straight.

   Aurel. Agreed, then lets go.   *Exeunt*

      Enter *Sander and his Mistres.*

  San. Come Mistris.

  Kate. *Sander* I prethe helpe me to some meate,
I am so faint that I can scarsely stande.

  San. I marry mistris but you know my maister
Has giuen me a charge that you must eate nothing,
But that which he himselfe giueth you.

  Kate. Why man thy Maister needs neuer know it.

  San. You say true indede: why looke you Mistris,
What say you to a peese of beeffe and mustard now?

  Kate. Why I say tis excellent meate, canst thou
helpe me to some?

  San. I, I could helpe you to some but that
I doubt the mustard is too collerick for you,
But what say you to a sheepes head and garlick?

  Kate. Why any thing, I care not what it be.

  San. I but the garlike I doubt will make your breath
stincke, and then my Maister will course me for letting
You eate it: But what say you to a fat Capon?

  Kate. Thats meate for a King sweet *Sander* helpe
Me to some of it.

  San. Nay berlady then tis too deere for vs, we must

                    Not

31

Not meddle with the Kings meate.

   Kate Out villaine dost thou mocke me,   960
Take that for thy sawsinesse.

         She beates him.

   San. Sounes are you so light fingerd with a murrin,
Ile keepe you fasting for it this two daies.

   Kate. I tell thee villaine Ile tear the flesh of
Thy face and eate it and thou prates to me thus.

   San. Here comes my Maister now hele course you.

      Enter *Ferando* with a peece of meate vppon his
        daggers point and *Polidor* with him.

   Feran. Se here *Kate* I haue prouided meate for thee,   970
Here take it: what ist not worthie thankes,
Goe sirra? take it awaie againe you shalibe
Thankefull for the next you haue.

   Kate Why I thanke you for it.

   Feran. Nay now tis not worth a pin go sirray and take
It hence I say.

   San. Yes sir Ile Carrie it hence: Maister let her
Haue none for she can fight as hungrie as she is.

   Pol. I pray you sir let it stand, for Ile eate
Some with her my selfe.

   Feran. Well sirra set it downe againe.   980

   Kate. Nay nay I pray you let him take it hence,
And keepe it for your owne diete for Ile none,
Ile nere be beholding to you for your Meate,
I tell thee flatlie here vnto the thy teethe
Thou shalt not keepe me nor feede me as thou list,
For I will home againe vnto my fathers house.

   Feran. I, when your meeke and gentell but not
Before, I know your stomack is not yet come downe,
Therefore no maruell thou canste not eate,
And I will goe vnto your Fathers house,   990
Come *Polidor* let vs goe in againe,

                             And

The taming of a Shrew.

And *Kate* come in with vs I know ere longe,
That thou and I shall louingly agree.   *Ex. Omnes*

Enter *Aurelius Valeria and Phylotus*
the Marchant.

Aurel. Now Senior *Phylotus*, we will go
Vnto *Alfonsos* house, and be sure you say
As I did tell you, concerning the man
That dwells in *Cestus*, whose son I said I was,
For you doo very much resemble him,
And feare not: you may be bold to speake your mind.

    Phylo. I warrant you sir take you no care,
Ile vse my selfe so cunning in the cause,
As you shall soone inioie your harts delight.

    Aurel. Thankes sweet *Phylotus*, then stay you here,
And I will go and fetch him hither straight.
Ho, Senior *Alfonso*: a word with you.

Enter *Alfonso.*   (matter
    Alfon. Whose there? what *Aurelius* whats the
That you stand so like a stranger at the doore?

    Aurel. My father sir is newly come to towne,
And I haue brought him here to speake with you,
Concerning those matters that *I* tolde you of,
And he can certefie you of the truth.

    Alfon. Is this your father? you are welcome sir.

    Phylo. Thankes *Alfonso*, for thats your name *I* gesse,
I vnderstand my son hath set his mind
And bent his liking to your daughters loue,
And for because he is my only son,
And I would gladly that he should doo well,
I tell you sir, I not mislike his choise,
If you agree to giue him your consent,
He shall haue liuing to maintaine his state,

E   Three

33

Three hundred poundes a yeere I will assure
To him and to his heyres, and if they do ioyne,
And knit themselues in holy wedlock bande,
A thousand massie in gots of pure gold,
And twise as many bares of siluer plate,
I freely giue him, and in writing straight,
I will confirme what I haue said in wordes.

Alfon. Trust me I must commend your liberall mind,
And louing care you beare vnto your son,
And here I giue him freely my consent,
As for my daughter I thinke he knowes her mind,
And I will inlarge her dowrie for your sake.
And solemnise with ioie your nuptiall rites,
But is this gentleman of *Cestus* too?

Aurel. He is the *Duke* of *Cestus* thrise renowned son,
Who for the loue his honour beares to me:
Hath thus accompanied me to this place.

Alfonso. You weare to blame you told me not before,
Pardon me my Lord, for if I had knowne
Your honour had bin here in place with me,
I would haue donne my dutie to your honour.

Val. Thankes good *Alfonso*: but I did come to see
When as these marriage rites should be performed,
And if in these nuptialls you vouchsafe,
To honour thus the prince of *Cestus* frend,
In celebration of his spousall rites,
He shall remaine a lasting friend to you,
What saies *Aurelius* father.

Phylo. I humbly thanke your honour good my Lord,
And ere we parte before your honor here:
Shall articles of such content be drawne,
As twixt our houses and postesities,
Eternallie this league of peace shall last,
Inuiolat and pure on either part:

Alfonso

1030

1040

1050

Alfonso. With all my heart, and if your honour please,
To walke along with vs vnto my house,
We will confirme these leagues of lasting loue.
Val. Come then *Aurelius* I will go with you. *Ex. omnes.*

Enter *Ferando and Kate and Sander.*
San. Master the haberdasher has brought my
Mistresse home her cappe here.
Feran. Come hither sirra: what haue you there?
Habar. A veluet cappe sir and it please you.
Feran. Who spoake for it? didst thou *Kate?*
Kate. What if I did, come hither sirra, giue me
The cap, Ile see if it will fit me.

She sets it one hir head.
Feran. O monstrous: why it becomes thee not,
Let me see it *Kate:* here sirra take it hence,
This cappe is out of fashion quite.
Kate The fashion is good inough: belike you,
Meane to make a foole of me.
Feran. Why true he meanes to make a foole of thee,
To haue thee put on such a curtald cappe,
sirra begon with it.

Enter the *Taylor* with a gowne.
San. Here is the *Taylor* too with my Mistris gowne.
Feran. Let me see it *Taylor:* what with cuts and iagges?
Sounes you villaine, thou hast spoiled the gowne. (tion,
Taylor. Why sir I made it as your man gaue me direc-
You may reade the note here.
Feran. Come hither sirra: *Taylor* reade the note.
Taylor. Item a faire round compast cape.
San. I thats true.
Taylor. And a large truncke sleeue.

E 2   *Sander*

San. Thats a lie maifter, I fayd two truncke fleeues.   1090
Feran. Well fir goe forward.
Tailor. Item a loofe bodied gowne.
San. Maifter if euer I fayd loofe bodies gowne,
Sew me in a feame and beate me to death,
With a bottome of browne thred.
Tailor. I made it as the note bad me.
San. I fay the note lies in his throate and thou too,
*A*nd thou fayft it.
Taylor. Nay nay nere be fo hot firra, for I feare you not.
San. Dooft thou heare *Taylor*,thou haft braued   1100
Many men: braue not me.
Thou'ft fafte many men.
Taylor. Well fir.
San. Face not me Ile nether be fafte nor braued
At thy handes I can tell thee.
Kate. Come come I like the fafhion of it well enough,
Heres more a do then needs Ile haue it I,
And if you do not like it hide your eies,
I thinke I fhall haue nothing by your will.
Feran. Go I fay and take it vp for your maifters vfe.   1110
San. Souns: villaine not for thy life touch it not,
Souns, take vp my miftris gowne to his
Maifters vfe?
Feran. Well fir: whats your conceit of it.
San. I haue a deeper conceite in it then you
thin'ke for, take vp my Miftris gowne
To his maifters vfe?
Feran. Tailor come hether: for this time take it
Hence againe, and Ile content thee for thy paines.
Taylor. I thanke you fir.   *Exit Taylor.*   1120
Feran. Come *Kate* we now will go fee thy fathers houfe
Euen in thefe honeft meane abilliments,
Our purfes fhallbe rich, our garments plaine,

                                          To

36

To shrowd our bodies from the winter rage,
And thats inough, what should we care for more.
Thy sisters *Kate* to morrow must be wed,
And I haue promised them thou shouldst be there
The morning is well vp lets hast away,
It will be nine a clocke ere we come there.

    Kate. Nine a clock, why tis allreadie past two
In the after noone by all the clocks in the towne.
    Feran. I say tis but nine a clock in the morning.
    Kate. I say tis tow a clock in the after noone.
    Feran. It shall be nine then ere we go to your fathers,
Come backe againe, we will not go to day.
Nothing but crossing of me still,
Ile haue you say as I doo ere you go.   *Exeunt omnes.*

    Enter *Polidor*, *Emelia*, *Aurelius and Philema.*
    Pol. Faire *Emelia* sommers sun bright Queene,
Brighter of hew then is the burning clime,
Where *Phœbus* in his bright æquator sits,
Creating gold and pressious minneralls,
What would *Emelia* doo? if I were forst
To leaue faire *Athens* and to range the world.
    Eme. Should thou assay to scale the seate of Ioue,
Mounting the suttle ayrie regions
Or be snacht vp as erste was *Ganimed*,
Loue should giue winges vnto my swift desires,
And prune my thoughts that I would follow thee,
Or fall and perish as did *Icarus*.
    Aurel. Sweetly resolued faire *Emelia*,
But would *Phylema* say as much to me,
If I should aske a question now of thee,
What if the duke of *Cestus* only son,
Which came with me vnto your fathers house,
Should seeke to git *Phylemas* loue from me,

                      And

And make thee Duches of that stately towne,
Wouldst thou not then forsake me for his loue?
   Phyle. Not for great *Neptune*, no nor *Ioue* himselfe,
Will *Phylema* leaue *Aurelius* loue,
Could he install me *Empres* of the world,
Or make me Queene and guidres of the heauens,
Yet would *I* not exchange thy loue for his,
Thy company is poore *Philemas* heauen,
And without thee, heauen were hell to me.
   Eme. And should my loue as erste did *Hercules*
Attempt to passe the burning valtes of hell,
I would with piteous lookes and pleasing wordes,
As once did *Orpheus* with his harmony,
And rauishing sound of his melodious harpe,
Intreate grim *Pluto* and of him obtaine,
That thou mightest go and safe retourne againe.
   Phyle. And should my loue as earst *Leander* did,
Attempte to swimme the boyling helispont
For *Heros* loue: no towers of brasse should hold
But I would follow thee through those raging flouds,
With lockes disheuered and my brest all bare,
With bended knees vpon *Abidas* shoore,
I would with smokie sighes and brinish teares,
Importune *Neptune* and the watry Gods,
To send a guard of siluer scaled *Dolphyns*,
With sounding *Tritons* to be our conuoy,
And to transport vs safe vnto the shore,
Whilst I would hang about thy louely necke,
Redoubling kisse on kisse vpon thy cheekes,
And with our pastime still the swelling waues.
   Eme. Should *Polidor* as great *Achilles* did,
Onely imploy himselfe to follow armes,
Like to the warlike *Amazonian* Queene,
Penthesilea Hectors paramore,
                                Who

1160
1170
1180
1190

The taming of a Shrew

Who foyld the bloudie *Pirrhus* murderous greeke,
Ile thruft my felfe amongft the thickeft throngs,
And with my vtmoft force affift my loue.

  Phyle. Let *Eole* ftorme: be mild and quiet thou,
Let *Neptune* fwell, be *Aurelius* calme and pleafed,
I care not I, betide what may betide,
Let fates and fortune doo the worft they can,
I recke them not: they not difcord with me,
Whilft that my loue and *I* do well agree·

  Aurel. Sweet *Phylema* bewties mynerall,
From whence the fun exhales his glorious fhine,
And clad the heauen in thy reflected raies,
And now my liefeft loue, the time drawes nie,
That *Himen* mounted in his faffron robe,
Muft with his torches waight vpon thy traine,
As *Hellens* brothers on the horned Moone,
Now *Iuno* to thy number fhall I adde,
The faireft bride that euer Marchant had.

  Pol. Come faire *Emelia* the preefte is gon,
And at the church your father and the refte,
Do ftay to fee our marriage rites performde,
And knit in fight of heauen this *Gordian* knot.
That teeth of fretting time may nere vntwift,
Then come faire loue and gratulate with me,
This daies content and fweet folemnity.   *Ex. Omnes*

  Slie Sim muft they be married now?
  Lord. *I* my Lord.

      Enter *Ferando and Kate and Sander.*
  Slie. Looke *Sim* the foole is come againe now.
  Feran. Sirra go fetch our horffes forth, and bring
Them to the backe gate prefentlie.

  San. I will fir *I* warrant you,   *Exit Sander.*
  Feran. Come *Kate* the Moone fhines cleere to night
methinkes.   *Kate.*

Kate. The moone? why husband you are deceiud
It is the fun.

Feran. Yet againe: come backe againe it fhall be
The moone ere we come at your fathers.

Kate. Why Ile fay as you fay it is the moone.

Feran. Iefus faue the glorious moone.

Kate. Iefus faue the glorious moone.

Feran. I am glad *Kate* your ftomack is come downe,
I know it well thou knoweft it is the fun,
But I did trie to fee if thou wouldft fpeake,
And croffe me now as thou haft donne before,
And truft me *kate* hadft thou not named the moone,
We had gon back againe as fure as death,
But foft whofe this thats comming here.

Enter the *Duke of Ceftus* alone.

Duke. Thus all alone from *Ceftus* am I come,
And left my princelie courte and noble traine,
To come to *Athens*, and in this difguife,
To fee what courfe my fon *Aurelius* takes,
But ftay, heres fome it may be Trauells thether,
Good fir can you dere&ct; me the way to *Athens?*

Ferando fpeakes to the olde man.
Fairé louely maide yoong and affable,
More cleere of hew and far more beautifull,
Then pretious *Sardonix* or purple rockes,
Of *Amithefts* or gliftering *Hiafinthe*,
More amiable farre then is the plain,
Where gliftring *Cepherus* in filuer boures,
Gafeth vpon the Giant *Andromede*,
Sweet *Kate* entertaine this louely woman.

Duke. I thinke the man is mad he calles me a woman.

Kate

1230

1240

1250

Kate. Faire louely lady, bright and Chriftalline,
Bewteous and ftately as the eie-traind bird,
As glorious as the morning wafht with dew,
Within whofe eies fhe takes her dawningbeames,
And golden fommer fleepes vpon thy cheekes,
Wrap vp thy radiations in fome cloud,
Leaft that thy bewty make this ftately towne,
Inhabitable like the burning *Zone*,
With fweet reflections of thy louely face.
   Duke. What is fhe mad to? or is my fhape transformd,
That both of them perfwade me I am a woman,
But they are mad fure, and therefore Ile begon,
And leaue their companies for fear of harme,
And vnto *Athens* haft to feeke my fon.
            Exit Duke.

   Feran. Why fo *Kate* this was friendly done of thee,
And kindly too: why thus muft we two liue,
One minde, one heart, and one content for both,
This good old man dos thinke that we are mad,
And glad he is I am fure, that he is gonne,
But come fweet *Kate* for we will after him,
And now perfwade him to his fhape againe.
            Ex. omnes.
    Enter *Alfonfo and Phylotus and Valeria,*
    Polidor, Emelia, Aurelius and Phylema.

   Alfon. Come louely fonnes your marriage rites
performed,
Lets hie vs home to fee what cheere we haue,
I wonder that *Ferando* and his wife
Comes not to fee this great folemnitie.
   Pol. No maruell if *Ferando* be away,
His wife I think hath troubled fo his wits,
        F   That

1260
1270
1280

That he remaines at home to keepe them warme,
For forward wedlocke as the prouerbe sayes,
Hath brought him to his nightcappe long agoe.

   Phylo. But *Polidor* let my son and you take heede,
That *Ferando* say not ere long as much to you,
And now *Alfonso* more to shew my loue,
If vnto *Cestus* you do send your ships,
My selfe will fraught them with *Arabian* silkes,
Rich affrick spices *Arras* counter poines,
Muske *Cassia:* sweet smelling *Ambergreece*,
Pearle, curroll, christall, iett, and iuorie,
To gratulate the fauors of my son,
And friendly loue that you haue shone to him.

   Vale. And for to honour him and this faire bride,
            Enter the Duke of Cestus.
Ile yerly send you from my fathers courte,
Chests of refind suger seuerally,
Ten tunne of tunis wine, sucket sweet druges,
To celibrate and solemnise this day,
And custome free your marchants shall conuerse:
And interchange the profits of your land,
Sending you gold for brasse, siluer for leade,
Casses of silke for packes of woll and cloth,
To binde this friendship and confirme this league.

   Duke. I am glad sir that you would be so franke,
Are you become the *Duke* of *Cestus* son,
And reuels with my treasure in the towne,
Base villaine that thus dishonorest me.

   Val. Sounes it is the *Duke* what shall I doo,
Dishonour thee why, knowst thou what thou saist?

   Duke. Her's no villaine: he will not know me now,
But what say you? haue you forgot me too?

   Phylo. Why sir, are you acquainted with my son?
   Duke. With thy son? no trust me if he be thine,

1290

1300

1310

1320

I

I pray you sir who am I?

Aurel. Pardon me father: humblie on my knees,
I do intreat your grace to heare me speake.

Duke. Peace villaine: lay handes on them,
And send them to prison straight.

          Phylotus and *Valeria* runnes away.

          Then *Slie* speakes.

Slie. I say wele haue no sending to prison.

Lord. My Lord this is but the play, theyre but in iest.

Slie. I tell thee *Sim* wele haue no sending,
To prison thats flat: why *Sim* am not I *Don Christo Vary?*
Therefore *I* say they shall not go to prison.

Lord. No more they shall not my Lord,
They be run away.

Slie. Are they run away *Sim?* thats well,
Then gis some more drinke, and let them play againe.

Lord. Here my Lord.

      Slie drinkes and then falls a sleepe.

Duke. Ah trecherous boy that durst presume,
To wed thy selfe without thy fathers leaue,
I sweare by fayre *Cinthea*s burning rayes,
By *Merops* head and by seauen mouthed *Nile,*
Had I but knowne ere thou hadst wedded her,
Were in thy brest the worlds immortall soule,
This angrie sword should rip thy hatefull chest,
And hewd thee smaller then the *Libian* sandes,
Turne hence thy face: oh cruell impious boy,
Alfonso I did not thinke you would presume,
To mach your daughter with my princely house,
And nere make me acquainted with the cause:

Alfon. My Lord by heauens I sweare vnto your grace,
I knew none other but *Valeria* your man,
Had bin the *Duke* of *Cestus* noble son,

      F 2   Nor

Nor did my daughter I dare sweare for her.

    Duke. That damned villaine that hath deluded me,
Whome I did send guide vnto my son,
Oh that my furious force could cleaue the earth,
That I might muster bands of hellish seendes,
To rack his heart and teare his impious soule.
The ceaselesse turning of celestiall orbes,
Kindles not greater flames in flitting aire,
Then passionate anguish of my raging brest,

    Aurel. Then let my death sweet father end your griefe,
For I it is that thus haue wrought your woes,
Then be reuengd on me for here I sweare,
That they are innocent of what I did,
Oh had I charge to cut of *Hydraes* hed,
To make the toplesse *Alpes* a champion field,
To kill vntamed monsters with my sword,
To trauell dayly in the hottest sun,
And watch in winter when the nightes be colde,
I would with gladnesse vndertake them all,
And thinke the paine but pleasure that I felt,
So that my noble father at my returne,
Would but forget and pardon my offence,

    Phile. Let me intreat your grace vpon my knees,
To pardon him and let my death discharge
The heauy wrath your grace hath vowd gainst him.

    Pol. And good my Lord let vs intreat your grace,
To purge your stomack of this Melancholy,
Taynt not your princely minde with griefe my Lord,
But pardon and forgiue these louers faults,
That kneeling craue your gratious fauor here.

    Emel. Great prince of *Cestus,* let a womans wordes,
Intreat a pardon in your lordly brest,
Both for your princely son, and vs my Lord.

    Duke. *Aurelius* stand vp I pardon thee,

I

I see that vertue will haue enemies,
And fortune willbe thwarting honour still,
And you faire virgin too I am content,
To accept you for my daughter since tis don,
And see you princely vsde in *Cestus* courte.

    Phyle. Thankes good my Lord and I no longer liue,
Then *I* obey and honour you in all:

    Alfon. Let me giue thankes vnto your royall grace,
For this great honor don to me and mine,
And if your grace will walke vnto my house,
I will in humblest maner I can, show
The eternall seruice I doo owe your grace.

    Duke Thanks good *Alfonso*: but I came alone,
And not as did beseeme the *Cestian Duke*,
Nor would I haue it knowne within the towne,
That I was here and thus without my traine,
But as I came alone so will I go,
And leaue my son to solemnise his feast,
And ere't belong Ile come againe to you,
And do him honour as beseemes the son
Of mightie *Ierobell* the *Cestian Duke*,
Till when Ile leaue you, Farwell *Aurelius*.

    Aurel. Not yet my Lord, Ile bring you to your ship.

                Exeunt Omnes.

                Slie sleepes.

    Lord. Whose within there? come hither sirs my Lords
A sleepe againe: go take him easily vp,
And put him in his one apparell againe,
And lay him in the place where we did find him,
Iust vnderneath the alehouse side below,
But see you wake him not in any case.

    Boy. It shall be don my Lord come helpe to beare him
      hence,   *Exit.*

              F 3   Enter

Enter *Ferando, Aurelius and Polidor*
and his boy and *Valeria and Sander.*

Feran. Come gentlemen now that suppers donne,
How shall we spend the time till we go to bed?
Aurel. Faith if you will in triall of our wiues,
Who will come sownest at their husbands call.
Pol. Nay then *Ferando* he must needes sit out,
For he may call I thinke till he be weary,
Before his wife will come before she list.
Feran. Tis well for you that haue such gentle wiues,
Yet in this triall will I not sit out,
It may be *Kate* will come as soone as yours.
Aurel. My wife comes soonest for a hundred pound.
Pol. I take it: Ile lay as much to youres,
That my wife comes as soone as I do send.
Aurel. How now *Ferando* you dare not lay belike.
Feran. Why true I dare not lay indeede;
But how, so little mony on so sure a thing,
A hundred pound: why I haue layd as much
Vpon my dogge, in running at a Deere,
She shall not come so farre for such a trifle,
But will you lay fiue hundred markes with me,
And whose wife soonest comes when he doth call,
And shewes her selfe most louing vnto him,
Let him inioye the wager I haue laid,
Now what say you? dare you aduenture thus?
Pol. I weare it a thousand pounds I durst presume
On my wiues loue: and *I* will lay with thee.

Enter *Alfonso.*

Alfon. How now sons what in conference so hard,
May I without offence, know where abouts.

Aurelius

1430

1440

1450

Aurel. Faith father a waighty caufe about our wiues
Fiue hundred markes already we haue layd,
And he whofe wife doth fhew moft loue to him,
He muft inioie the wager to himfelfe.

Alfon. Why then *Ferando* he is fure to lofe,
I promife thee fon thy wife will hardly come,
And therefore I would not wifh thee lay fo much.

Feran. Tufh father were it ten times more,
I durft aduenture on my louely *Kate,*
But if I lofe Ile pay, and fo fhall you.

Aurel. Vpon mine honour if I loofe Ile pay.

Pol. And fo will I vpon my faith I vow.

Feran. Then fit we downe and let vs fend for them.

Alfon. I promife thee *Ferando* I am afraid thou wilt lofe

Aurel. Ile fend for my wife firft, *Valeria*
Go bid your Miftris come to me.

Val. I will my Lord.

Exit Valeria.

Aurel. Now for my hundred pound.
Would any lay ten hundred more with me,
I know I fhould obtaine it by her loue.

Feran. I pray God you haue not laid too much already.

Aurel. Truft me *Ferando* I am fure you haue,
For you I dare prefume haue loft it all.

Enter *Valeria* againe.

Now firra what faies your miftris?

Val. She is fomething bufie but fhele come anon.

Feran. Why fo, did not I tell you this before,
She is bufie and cannot come.   (fwere

Aurel. I pray God your wife fend you fo good an an-
She may be bufie yet fhe fayes fhele come.

Feran. Well well: *Polidor* fend you for your wife.

Polidor

47

Pol. Agreed·*Boy* defire your miftris to come hither.
Boy. I will fir   *Ex. Boy.*
Feran. I fo fo he defiers her to come.
Alfon. Polidor I dare prefume for thee,
I thinke thy wife will not deny to come.
And I do maruel'l much *Aurelius,*   1490
That your wife came not when you fent for her.

                    Enter the *Boy* againe.

Pol. Now wheres your Miftris?
Boy. She bad me tell you that fhe will not come,
And you haue any bufineffe, you muft come to her.
Feran. Oh monftrous intollerable prefumption,
Worfe then a blafing ftarre, or fnow at midfommer,
Earthquakes or any thing vnfeafonable,
She will not come: but he muft come to her.
Pol. Well fir *I* pray you lets here what   1500
Anfwere your wife will make.
Feran. Sirra, command your Miftris to come
To me prefentlie.   *Exit Sander.*
Aurel. I thinke my wife for all fhe did not come,
Will proue moft kinde for now I haue no feare,
For I am fure *Ferandos* wife, fhe will not come.
Feran. The mores the pittie: then I muft lofe.
                    Enter *Kate* and *Sander.*
But I haue won for fee where *Kate* doth come.
Kate. Sweet husband did you fend for me?   1510
Feran. I did my loue I fent for thee to come,
Come hither *Kate,* whats that vpon thy head
Kate. Nothing husband but my cap I thinke.
Feran. Pull it of and treade it vnder thy feete,
*T*is foolifh I will not haue thee weare it.
                    She takes of her cap and treads on it.

                                        Polidor

Pol. Oh wonderfull metamorphosis.

Aurel. This is a wonder: almost past beleefe.

Feran. This is a token of her true loue to me,
And yet Ile trie her further you shall see,
Come hither *Kate* where are thy sisters.

Kate. They be sitting in the bridall chamber.

Feran. Fetch them hither and if they will not come,
Bring them perforce and make them come with thee.

Kate. I will.

Alfon. I promise thee *Ferando* I would haue sworne,
Thy wife would nere haue donne so much for thee.

Feran. But you shall see she will do more then this,
For see where she brings her sisters forth by force.

Enter *Kate* thrusting *Phylema* and *Emelia* before her,
and makes them come vnto their husbands call.

Kate See husband I haue brought them both.

Feran. Tis well don *Kate*.

Eme. I sure and like a louing peece, your worthy
To haue great praise for this attempt.

Phyle. I for making a foole of her selfe and vs.

Aurel. Beshrew thee *Phylema*, thou hast
Lost me a hundred pound to night.
For I did lay that thou wouldst first haue come.

Pol. But thou *Emelia* hast lost me a great deale more.

Eme. You might haue kept it better then,
Who bad you lay?

Feran. Now louely *Kate* before there husbands here,
I prethe tell vnto these hedstrong women,
What dutie wiues doo owe vnto their husbands.

Kate. Then you that liue thus by your pompered wills,
Now list to me and marke what I shall say,
Theternall power that with his only breath,
Shall cause this end and this beginning frame,

G   Not

49

Not in time, nor before time, but with time, confusd,   1550
For all the course of yeares, of ages, moneths,
Of seasons temperate, of dayes and houres,
Are tund and stopt, by measure of his hand,
The first world was, a forme, without a forme,
A heape confusd a mixture all deformd,
A gulfe of gulfes, a body bodiles,
Where all the elements were orderles,
Before the great commander of the world;
The King of Kings the glorious God of heauen,
Who in six daies did frame his heauenly worke,   1560
And made all things to stand in perfit course.
Then to his image he did make a man.
Olde *Adam* and from his side a sleepe,
A rib was taken, of which the Lord did make,
The woe of man so termd by *Adam* then,
Woman for that, by her came sinne to vs,
And for her sin was *Adam* doomd to die,
As *Sara* to her husband, so should we,
Obey them, loue them, keepe, and nourish them,
If they by any meanes doo want our helpes,   1570
Laying our handes vnder theire feete to tread,
If that by that we, might procure there ease,
And for a president Ile first begin,
And lay my hand vnder my husbands feete
    She laies her hand vnder her husbands feete.
Feran. Inough sweet, the wager thou hast won,
And they I am sure cannot denie the same.
    Alfon. I Ferando the wager thou hast won,
And for to shew thee how *I* am pleasd in this,
A hundred poundes I freely giue thee more,   1580
Another dowry for another daughter,
For she is not the same she was before.
    Feran. Thankes sweet father, gentlemen godnight
                               For

For *Kate* and *I* will leaue you for to night,
Tis *Kate* and I am wed, and you are sped.
And so farwell for we will to our beds.

Exit Ferando and Kate and Sander.

Alfon. Now *Aurelius* what say you to this?
Aurel. Beleeue me father I reioice to see,
Ferando and his wife so louingly agree.

Exit Aurelius and Phylema and
Alfonso and Valeria.

Eme. How now *Polidor* in a dump, what sayst thou
man?
Pol. I say thou art a shrew.
Eme. Thats better then a sheepe.
Pol. Well since tis don let it go, come lets in.

Exit Polidor and Emelia.

Then enter two bearing of *Slie* in his
Owne apparrell againe, and leaues him
Where they found him, and then goes out.
Then enter the *Tapster.*

Tapster. Now that the darkesome night is ouerpast,
And dawning day apeares in cristall sky,
Now must I hast abroad: but soft whose this?
What *Slie* oh wondrous hath he laine here allnight,
Ile wake him, I thinke he's starued by this,
But that his belly was so stuft with ale,
What how *Slie*, Awake for shame.
Slie. *Sim* gis some more wine: whats all the
Plaiers gon: am not I a Lord?
Tapster. A Lord with a murrin: come art thou
dronken still?
Slie. Whose this? *Tapster*, oh Lord sirra, I haue had
The brauest dreame to night, that euer thou
Hardest in all thy life.

Tapster

1590
1600
1610

Tapster. I marry but you had best get you home,
For your wife will course you for dreming here to night,
Slie Will she? I know now how to tame a shrew,
I dreamt vpon it all this night till now,
And thou hast wakt me out of the best dreame
That euer I had in my life, but Ile to my
Wife presently and tame her too
And if she anger me.
Tapster. Nay tarry *Slie* for Ile go home with thee,
And heare the rest that thou hast dreamt to night.

Exeunt Omnes.

FINIS.